OKANAGAN UNIVERSITY COLLEGE
LIBRARY
BRITISH COLUMBIA

D0198674

K

Awesome Experiments in

Light
&Sound

Michael DiSpezio

Illustrations by Catherine Leary

Sterling Publishing Co., Inc
New York

ACKNOWLEDGMENTS

Again, I have had the wonderful opportunity to work with my Sterling team on this brand-new series of science books. I'd like to acknowledge the dedication and ability of my energetic and always upbeat editor, Hazel Chan, and the talent and kid-friend style of artist Catherine Leary. I'd also like to recognize Sheila Barry for nurturing and encouraging this series from its conception.

In addition, there are many instructors, colleagues, and friends who have unselfishly shared their expertise and wide-ranging experiences acquired in the "trenches" of science education. It is their thoughts, conceptualizations, explanations, and passion that continually sculpt my teaching style, writing, and philosophy.

I'd also like to thank my son, Anthony, for helping me tweak these experiments and continually see the world through the eyes of a child!

Library of Congress Cataloging-in-Publication Data

Dispezio, Michael A.
    Awesome experiments in light & sound / by Michael Dispezio ;
illustrated by Catherine Leary.
      p.   cm.
    Includes index.
    Summary: Presents over seventy experiments designed to demonstrate the properties of light and sound and explain the science behind them, covering such topics as wavelengths, color spectrums, vibration, and air particles.
    ISBN 0-8069-9823-7
    1. Light—Experiments—Juvenile literature. 2. Sound—Experiments—Juvenile literature. [1. Light—Experiments. 2. Sound—Experiments. 3. Experiments.] I. Leary, Catherine, ill. II. Title. III. Title: Awesome experiments in light and sound.
QC360.D58   1999
535'.078—dc21   98-40845
                                                  CIP
                                                  AC

10 9 8 7 6 5 4 3 2 1

First paperback edition published in 2000 by
Sterling Publishing Company, Inc.
387 Park Avenue South, New York, N.Y. 10016
© 1999 by Michael DiSpezio
Distributed in Canada by Sterling Publishing
% Canadian Manda Group, One Atlantic Avenue, Suite 105
Toronto, Ontario, Canada M6K 3E7
Distributed in Great Britain and Europe by Chris Lloyd
463 Ashley Road, Parkstone, Poole, Dorset, BH14 0AX, England
Distributed in Australia by Capricorn Link (Australia) Pty Ltd.
P.O. Box 6651, Baulkham Hills, Business Centre, NSW 2153, Australia
Manufactured in the United States of America
All rights reserved

Sterling ISBN 0-8069-9823-7 Trade
              0-8069-9311-1 Paper

C O N T E N T S

PART TWO
SOUND

SAFETY FIRST

Follow all instructions, cautions, and safety notes. To protect your eyes, wear safety goggles when performing all of the experiments. Conduct every experiment with proper supervision. Have an adult perform all steps that use a flame, wall outlet, sharp point, cutting edge, or any other potentially dangerous tool. Neither the author nor the publisher shall be liable for injuries that may be caused by not following the experiment steps or adhering to the safety notes.

INTRODUCTION

This book is a guide. Its primary purpose is to accompany you through more than seventy adventures in learning. As you perform these experiments, you'll celebrate the magic of science. You'll also observe how science isn't a distant notion limited to classrooms, laboratories, books, and PBS specials. Science is all around you!

Unlike many other subjects, science is constructed from inquiry. This philosophy of exploration is a cornerstone of the National Science Education Standards. It is also the premise upon which the *Awesome Experiments in Science* series has been created. With an increased focus on understanding (and NOT memorizing facts), these books offer kid-friendly experiments that will engage, harness, and nurture your thinking skills.

PART

ONE

LIGHT

1.1 CATCH THE RAYS

What do you think of when you hear the word "ray"?
  a. A vaporizing beam that is fired from a Martian spaceship.
  b. A strange-looking fish.
  c. A used car dealer from Fresno, California.
  d. Arrows that show the path that light travels along.

Although all of the above answers are correct, we'll *focus* on answer D. It's these types of ray that are used by scientists to show how light travels.

Materials

* *three index cards*
* *pair of scissors*
* *modeling clay*
* *flashlight*

To Do

Use a pair of scissors to cut a penny-sized hole in the middle of three index cards. Set each card into a base formed by a small lump of clay. Line the three cards in a row so that their holes are positioned in a straight line.

Shine the beam of a flashlight into the hole of the most distant card. Look through the hole of the card closest to you. What do you see? Can you describe the path of the light rays as they travel from the flashlight to your eyes?

Move the middle card about an inch to the side so that this card now blocks the path of light. What do you see now? What happened to the light? Can you find any trace of the light on the moved card? Explain your observation.

The Science

Light rays travel in a straight line. When the three holes were aligned, the rays traveled in a straight line from the flashlight to your eyes. When the middle card was moved, its surface got in the way of the beam. Since light travels in a straight line, it could not bend around the card. Instead, the beam was blocked from completing a path to your eye.

1.2 RAINBOW TRAY

White light is more than meets the eye. It's a mix of all the colors of the rainbow (red, orange, yellow, green, blue, and violet). These colors make up the visible spectrum. There are several ways that white light can be separated into its component colors. Here's one:

Materials
* small mirror
* tray
* water
* sheet of white paper

CAUTION
Do not look directly at the Sun or at the Sun's reflected image in the surface of the mirror.

To Do
Fill a tray with water. Set the tray in bright sunlight. Position a mirror inside at one end of the tray. The mirror should be set at an angle that is supported by the tray edge.

Look at the mirror's reflection that is cast upon a nearby surface. What do you see? To make the pattern appear brighter, place a sheet of white paper beneath its reflection.

The Science
Light travels in waves. Like ocean waves, it has high points called *crests* and low points called *troughs*. The distance from one crest to the next is a measurement called *wavelength*.

A beam of white light contains rays of many different wavelengths. Each wavelength has its own color. Red has the longest wavelength. Next comes orange, followed by yellow, green, and blue. Violet is the color with the shortest wavelength.

When white light is reflected through the mirror and water, it is separated into its component colors. The colors spread out as a side-by-side pattern we call a spectrum.

CHECK IT OUT! Take a look at the surface of a compact disk. Where do the rainbows come from?

LONG WAVE LENGTH

SHORT WAVE LENGTH

1.3 CLIFF-HANGER

Have you ever heard the term "cliff-hanger"? If so, you may know that it referred to the suspenseful final scene of a film or television show. The typical cliff-hanger was a situation in which a main character was placed in mortal danger—often hanging from a cliff. You had to tune in the following week to see if that person survived. In our version of a cliff-hanger, we'll skip the danger. Instead, we'll paint the scene with rainbows.

Materials
* stack of books
* drinking glass
* water
* flashlight
* clay

To Do
Fill a drinking glass one-third full of water. Position a stack of books on a flat surface. The stack should be slightly taller than an upright flashlight.

Place the water-filled glass on the top of the stack. Slide the glass so that a portion of it extends beyond the edge of the books, but it doesn't fall off.

Place the flashlight directly beneath the overhanging glass. You can put a small lump of clay at the base of the flashlight to prevent it from slipping. Turn on the flashlight and dim the lights in the room.

Look at the ceiling. What do you see?

Repeat the activity with a glass that is two-thirds full of water. Can you see any difference in the rainbow?

The Science
The beam of light struck the water-filled glass at a slight angle. This encounter separated the white light into its component colors. Although separated, these side-by-side colors continued on their deflected journey. Eventually, they struck the ceiling and produced a cool-looking spectrum.

1.4 COMPACT COLORS

One stores sounds. The other stores programs (which often include sounds). But even though their data is different, music and computer CDs are very similar. Both disks are storage mediums. They contain a huge amount of information stored in a code of tiny pits. And even though you can't see these pits, you can observe the great optical effects they produce!

Materials
* compact disk
* flashlight

To Do
Hold the CD by the edges of the disk (otherwise, you might scratch or damage the data). Examine both sides of the disk. Which side contains the stored information? How can you tell?

Hold the disk so that light reflects off its surface. What do you see? Gradually change the viewing angle. Do the rainbows change? Does the CD cast a rainbow shadow on a wall?

Hold a flashlight several feet from the CD. Aim the beam on the shiny surface. Can you find a reflected rainbow? Move the beam closer to the CD. Can you uncover any rainbow reflections?

The Science
The shiny surface of the CD contains an incredible number of closely spaced pits. The spacing is so close that their pattern can affect light. When white light falls on this surface, the colors separate out. The order of separation depends upon the color's wavelength. Colors with the longest wavelengths (red) bend the least. Those with shorter wavelengths (violet) bend the most. This bending produces spread-out bands of the spectrum.

1.5 SOAPY SPECTRUM

Have you ever looked at a film of oil floating on water? If so, did you see a swirling rainbow? The oil, like a mirror in water, separated white light into its component colors. In this next experiment, you'll replace the oil with bubble solution to get some colorful results.

Materials
* bubble solution
* small dish
* flashlight
* pipe cleaner
* tape
* sheet of white paper

To Do
Bend a pipe cleaner into a loop. Make sure to keep a small handle for holding the loop. Fill a dish with bubble solution.

Dip the loop into the bubble solution. Let the solution saturate the loop. After several minutes, gently remove the loop. What do you see? Are any colors present?

Tape a sheet of white paper on the wall. Dim the lights in the room.

Turn on the flashlight and aim its bright beam through the soapy loop. Position the flashlight so that the loop shadow is cast on the paper. Describe the shadow.

The Science
Very thin films can separate white light into its component colors. White light that passes through the bubble solution breaks apart into its spectrum. The separated light waves continue traveling and produce a colored shadow on the nearby wall.

CHECK IT OUT! Why do oil slicks often produce swirling rainbows?

1.6 RAINBOWS: THE NATURAL WAY

Have you ever shot the spray of a garden hose straight into the air? If the lighting was right, a rainbow may have appeared in the falling mist. Think back to the conditions needed to make this rainbow. Was the sun in front of you or behind you? In this experiment, you'll once again use a water mist to create a rainbow. Your water source, however, will be limited to a spray bottle.

Materials
* water bottle with spray top
* water
* bright light

To Do
Fill a water spray bottle with water. Stand outside on a bright sunny day and face away from the sun.

Hold the spray bottle in front of you. Aim high and pump out a continual mist of water. You may have to adjust the nozzle so that a fine mist is released.

Look into the falling mist. What do you see? How much of a rainbow can you observe? What color is on the inner side of the arc? What color is on the outermost side?

The Science
In order to see a rainbow, three conditions must be met: 1) The sun must be behind you. 2) You have to look away from the sun. 3) There have to be water droplets in the sky. If these conditions exist, then rainbows can appear.

Light that enters a water droplet bends slightly and separates into its component colors. When these colors strike the far surface of the droplet, they get reflected. When they eventually exit the droplet, the colors follow a final path that takes them to the observer's eye.

1.7 ADDING COLORS .

$\mathbb{T}$rue or false?

Every time you observe white, all of the colors of the spectrum are present.

Would you be surprised to learn that the answer is *false*? Your brain can be tricked into seeing white. This deception occurs when you view the right mix of certain colors and shades. Two color combinations, such as blue mixed with yellow or red mixed with bluish-green (called cyan), can also appear white.

Can other combinations produce the illusion of white? Read on.

Materials
* *three flashlights*
* *transparent plastic report covers (red, blue, and green)*
* *pair of scissors*
* *tape*

To Do
Obtain a red, blue, and green plastic report cover. Cut out a disk from each cover about the size of the flashlight lens.

Tape one disk over the clear lens of each flashlight. Aim the red beam at a nearby white wall. What color do you see?

While the red remains on, aim the beam of blue so that it overlaps half of the red spot. What happens?

Now aim the beam of green so that all three colors fall on the same spot. What happens as the colors are added to each other?

The Science
When light beams fall upon each other, the combined colors are added together. Unlike the mixing of paint pigments, this additive process produces lighter colors. When the right combination is produced, we "see" white.

Real World Connection
The next time that you're in a performance theater, take a look at the stage lights. Most likely, you'll see a row of lights that surround the

stage. These border lights aren't white. Instead, they consist of a pattern of colored lights. When projected, these different colors create white.

1.8 WHIRLING WHITE

Like it or not, your brain isn't that quick. When presented with a series of fast-changing animation frames, your brain can't see them as individual images. Instead, it blends them together. This inability to quickly "refresh" what you see is called persistence of vision. In this experiment, you'll use persistence of vision to create a slightly different effect.

Materials
* *heavy stock white paper*
* *pair of scissors*
* *colored markers (red, blue, and green)*
* *kite string*
* *pushpin*

To Do
Trace the pattern shown on the opposite page onto a sheet of heavy stock white paper. Use a pair of scissors to carefully cut out the circular shape.

Color one of the sections red. If possible use a red hue that has some yellow in it—or add a small "pie slice" of yellow.

Color the second section green. Color the third blue. Use a pushpin or other sharp point to punch two holes near the center of the circle.

Cut a length of string about 2 feet long. Thread the string through the holes and tie the loose ends together. Adjust the string so that two equal-sized loops are formed on both sides of the disk.

Gently pull on the ends of the loop. Then release the tension to allow the loops to wind up. Slowly pull the loops apart. Now let them come together. Apart, together. Apart, together.

Each time add a little more energy to the pull. Keep going until you've "worked" the disk into a whirling spin.

Look at the colored side. Can you still make out the individual colors? What happens to their appearance as the spin increases in speed?

The Science

When the disk is spinning, your eyes are stimulated by the red, blue, and green colors. At a fast enough rate, your brain can't separate these colors. Instead, the distinct regions have an additive effect and your brain interprets this mixture as white (or, more likely, some shade of light gray).

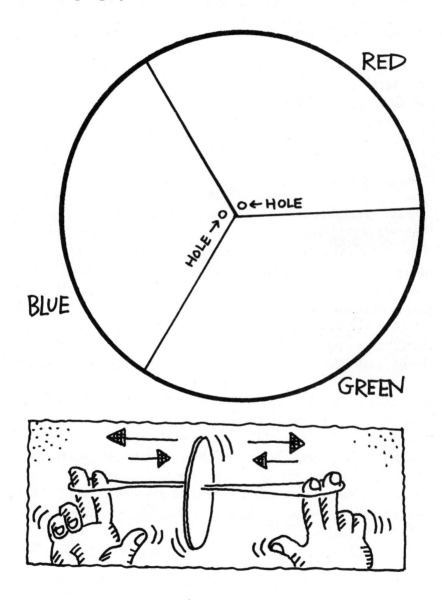

1.9 SCRATCH ANOTHER MIRROR

Throw a ball against a smooth wall. Most likely, you'll be able to predict the location of the ball's return bounce. Suppose you threw the ball against a rough or jagged wall. Would it be as easy to guess the spot of this return bounce? Why?

Materials
* discarded plastic CD case
* sandpaper
* water

To Do
Look into the clear plastic of a discarded (and soon to be destroyed) CD case. What do you see? What causes the surface of the plastic to produce this reflection?

Take a piece of sandpaper and rough up the surface of the CD. Look into the plastic again. What happened to the reflection?

Wet the rough surface with water. Does the reflective quality of the plastic change?

The Science
The original case's surface was smooth and slick. Light rays that struck this plastic were reflected in a uniform pattern (which retained the original image). Therefore, when you looked into the CD case, you observed your own reflection.

When the surface was rubbed with sandpaper, you created pits and scratches in the plastic. These rough features disrupted the reflection pattern and scattered the light beam's original image.

Placing water on the surface helped fill some of the holes. As the surface became smoother, it regained some of its reflective qualities.

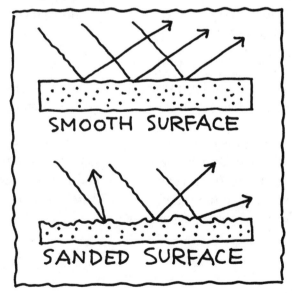

SMOOTH SURFACE

SANDED SURFACE

1.10 AS OTHERS SEE YOU

Look into a mirror and whom do you see? You? Is it the same you that others see? Pretty much, except that it is right/left reversed. When you look into a mirror, the right side of your face appears on the reflected image's left side. Hum, right-left, left-right? Is there a way of correcting it? !si ereht teb uoY

Materials
* *lipstick*
* *two mirrors*

To Do
Use lipstick to draw a small dot on your right cheek—your RIGHT cheek. Now look into a mirror. Study the reflected image. Suppose the image was someone else. On what cheek is the dot drawn?

Now blink your left eye. Your other left eye. Good. Again, study the reflected image. Which eye blinks?

Get a second mirror. Position the two mirrors so that your reflected image bounces between the two mirrored surfaces. You may have to adjust the angle. When the mirrors are positioned correctly, you'll see yourself as others see you.

The Science
Mirror images are right/left reversed. In order to reverse the reflection (and bring it back to normal), you need to double reflect the image.

Using the two mirrors, you built a double reflection system. Light from the lipstick spot first fell onto the opposite cheek in the first mirror. It reflected onto the second mirror. There it reversed a second time and went back to the correct cheek. This "corrected" image was the view that was detected by your eyes.

1.11 MIRROR TO MIRROR

Bathrooms are often great laboratories for exploring the properties of mirrors. The sink mirror reflects its image onto the door mirror. The door mirror reflects its image onto the shaving mirror. The shaving mirror reflects its image onto the make-up mirror. Pretty soon, you're not alone. The bathroom is now packed with thousands of people who look exactly like you—all trying to do science experiments!

Materials
* two mirrors
* coin
* small toy
* clay

To Do
Set two mirrors in a lump of clay. Position the mirrors so that they are about ½ foot apart.

Place a small toy between the two mirrors. Look into one mirror and count the number of toy images.

Guess how many toy images will appear in the other mirror. Once you've made your guess, check it out. Do both mirrors have the same image or does one show the toy slightly closer? Why?

Explore how tilting the mirrors and changing the distance between them affect the reflections.

The Science
The parallel mirrors create a pattern of reflection that produces an infinite number of reflected images. Each time the image was reflected, its light rays traveled back across the gap to the other mirror. There, this slightly smaller image was reflected back to the other mirror. Again and again and again and again a parade of shrinking images form!

1.12 JUST FOR FUN

What do the words book, hide, and box have in common? Think about it. Don't answer too quickly. Here's a hint. It has nothing to do with their meaning! Their likeness is based upon the appearance of their letters (or I should say half-letters). Give up?

Materials
- mirror
- clay
- pair of scissors
- paper
- markers

To Do
Cut out three rectangular scraps of paper. Print the word "BOX" on one of the rectangular paper, "HIKE" on another, and "COOKIE" on the third piece. Make sure to use ALL capital letters and write them along a straight line.

Once the words are written, use a pair of scissors to cut them in half (the top half of the word must be separated from the bottom half of the word). Discard the upper halves.

Place a mirror along the upper margin of the lower word half. Look into the mirror and what do you see? Why does this optical trick work? What other letters and words can be used?

The Science
Welcome to the science and "fun" of symmetry. The letters that were used in this experiment can be divided into identical upper and lower halves. Therefore, if one half is discarded, it can be replaced with the reflection of the lower half. The letters that have this type of symmetry include B, C, D, E, H, I K, O, and X.

1.13 REFLECTED RAYS

It's tool time. This tool, however, won't help you hammer nails into the wall or saw a board in half. It's a simple device that produces side-by-side light beams. By observing the behavior of these beams, you'll be able to learn more about the properties of light.

Materials
* index card
* comb
* pair of scissors
* tape
* flashlight
* mirror
* clay

To Do
To construct a "ray maker," cut a rectangular opening in the center of an index card's long edge. Use tape to secure a comb over this opening. Try to position the thicker comb's teeth in the opening. Bend back the side edges of the card so that it stands freely.

Secure a mirror with a small lump of clay. Set the upright mirror in the center of a table. Place the ray maker several inches from the mirror.

Flip on your flashlight. Aim the light beam through the teeth of the comb so that the light strikes the mirror. Observe what happens to these beams as they reflect off the mirror's surface. Do the beams change direction? How does the angle at which they strike the mirror compare to the angle at which they reflect off the mirror's surface?

The Science
Light that traveled through the openings between the comb teeth formed visible beams. These beams struck the surface of the mirror and were reflected. By examining the beams and their reflections, you can uncover how light behaves when it strikes a mirror.

CONNECTION: If you look closely, you'll observe that the light rays tend to spread out and become less concentrated. This spreading behavior is due to the type of light produced by the flashlight bulb. In contrast, LASER light is a special type of light that does not spread.

The rays of a LASER beam can remain parallel over interplanetary distances. In your home, however, LASERS are not practical tools. For these experiments, you'll have to accept the spread of the beam projector.

N O T E : Save this ray-making tool! You'll need it for several other experiments.

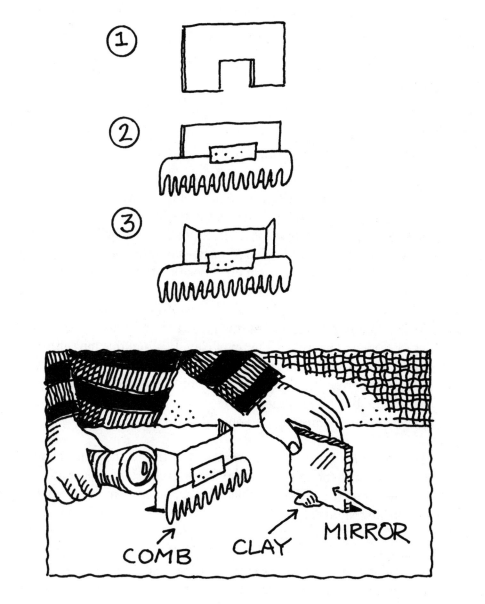

COMB   CLAY   MIRROR

1.14 BOUNCING AROUND

Most of the light that strikes a mirrored surface is not absorbed by the material. Instead, this light bounces off the reflective surface. Since the mirror is flat, the light rays are not randomly scattered. Instead, they travel together side-by-side as a reflected beam. This beam keeps traveling on a straight path until it strikes another surface.

Materials
* flashlight
* clay
* several small hand mirrors
* target bull's-eye
* tape

To Do
Draw a target bull's-eye. Use tape to attach the bull's-eye to the wall.

Dim the lights in the room. Turn on the flashlight. Aim the beam at the target. Not too hard to do, is it? Let's make this a little more difficult as you observe the reflective properties of mirrors.

Set a small mirror in a lump of clay. Position this mirror on a desktop. Aim your beam of light at the mirror. You may have to set the flashlight in some clay to secure its position. Adjust the mirror so that the flashlight's beam is reflected upon the target. Good.

Set up a second mirror in a lump of clay. Position this mirror a few feet away from the first mirror. Now adjust both mirrors so that the beam bounces from the first to the second. The final reflected beam should hit the bull's-eye target.

How many more mirrors can you add to this setup?

WITH OTHERS: You may want to try this with some friends. Instead of setting the mirrors in clay, have each friend hold a mirror. Then figure out the order in which the reflected beam must travel before striking a target.

The Science
Light that struck the mirror's surface was reflected in another direction. This reflected beam struck another mirror and was reflected

again. Eventually, the beam was projected onto the target. The target surface was not a mirror. It did, however, reflect light. This reflected "spot" was detected by your eyes.

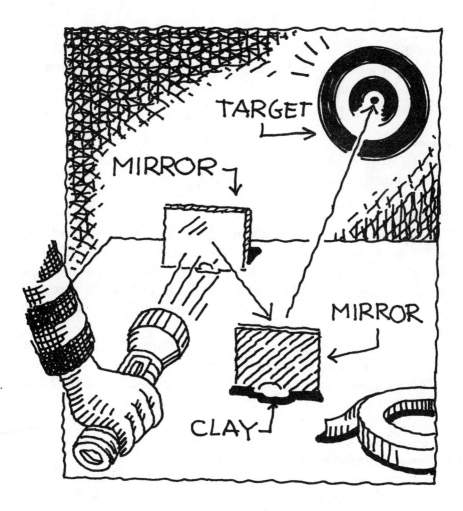

1.15 WHAT'S YOUR ANGLE?

Imagine trying to shoot a billiard ball against the side bumper of a pool table. If you shoot the ball so that it hits the cushion straight on, the ball bounces right back to where it came from. However, if you angle the path of the ball, it no longer comes right back. Instead, it is reflected in another direction. Right now, you may be wondering what do pool balls and light rays have in common. Keep reading. We'll reflect on that later.

Materials
* flashlight
* small mirror
* ruler
* tape

To Do
Use tape to place a set of marks along one wall of a hallway or narrow room. Place the first mark 1 foot above the floor. Place the second mark 1 foot above the first (2 feet high). Add two more marks, one at 3 feet high and the final one at 4 feet high. Make sure that when you position the marks, they are placed directly atop each other.

Place a mirror in the center of the hallway floor. The mirror should be placed in line with the set of wall marks.

Dim the lights in the hallway. Position your flashlight at the 1-foot mark. The back end of the flashlight should remain in contact with the wall. Aim the beam at the mirror. Observe where the reflected spot appears. Mark this spot with a piece of tape.

Position the flashlight at the other marks along this wall. Observe and mark where the reflected spot appears. How does the angle at which the flashlight beam strikes the mirror affect its reflection?

Suppose the beam came from directly above the mirror. Where would the reflected spot appear?

The Science
The angle at which the beam strikes the mirror determines the angle of reflection. If the striking beam (also called the incident beam) hits this surface at a shallow angle, the reflected beam will travel outward

along a shallow angle. Likewise, if the incident beam strikes the mirror at a steep angle, the reflected angle will also be steep.

In your hallway experiment, the spot always appeared on the opposite wall at the same height from which the beam began. Since the angle of the incident ray equaled the angle of the reflected ray, this spot had to appear at the same height.

1.16 REMOTE REFLECTION

Imagine life without a TV remote control unit. Horrible! But believe it or not, prior to the 1970s most television sets did not have remote control. In order to change the channel, a person had to stand up, walk to the TV, and manually turn the knob. Incredible.

Materials
* *TV with remote control*
* *mirror*

To Do
Switch on the television. Now use your remote control device to change channels. Determine how far away from the TV the remote can control it. Place a sheet of paper between the remote and the television. Does the remote still work or does the paper block the signal?

Stand about 10 feet from the television. Aim the remote at the side of the TV. How far away from the TV can the remote be aimed before it no longer switches channels?

Can the beam bounce off the ceiling and still reach the TV? Try reflecting the beam off the ceiling and wall. Will the beam be reflected off or absorbed by these surfaces?

Place a mirror on the floor about midway between you and the television. Hold the remote at the same height as the remote receiver on the television set. Aim the beam at the mirror. What happens? Can you explain your observation?

The Science
Although the remote control doesn't use visible light (otherwise we'd see the beam), it uses a similar form of energy called infrared light. Infrared, also called IR, has many of the properties of visible light. Like the colors we see, IR can bounce off mirrored surfaces. That's why the beam that struck the mirror changed the channel. Like visible light, it was reflected from the surface and traveled along a path that ended at the TV remote receiver.

1.17 MIRRORS IN THE HALL

R̲eflections can be confusing, especially when you are trying to find your way out of a funhouse. No matter where you look, a never-ending series of reflections look back. Only by feeling for an opening can you navigate through this maze of mirrors. In this next experiment, you'll build a much smaller, but equally confusing mirror hall.

Materials
* *three small plastic mirrors (with frames removed)*
* *coin*
* *clay*
* *pencil*
* *tape*

CAUTION
If you use glass mirrors, do not remove the glass from the frame. Exposed glass edges of these mirrors are extremely sharp.

To Do
Set the base of each mirror in a small lump of clay. Arrange two mirrors on a flat surface so that their sides form a right angle. Place a coin in the center of these two mirrors. Examine the coin's reflection in the mirrors. Change the angle at which the mirrors connect. How does this affect the reflected image?

Remove the coin. Add a third mirror so that a triangle is formed. Stand a pencil in a clay base. Position the pencil in the center of this tiny hall of mirrors. Peer into the middle and what do you see?

The Science
It's that mirror thing again. When you look into one of the mirrors, you see more than the object. You observe a reflection that is reflected and reflected and reflected. This multiple reflection produces a series of images that can appear endless.

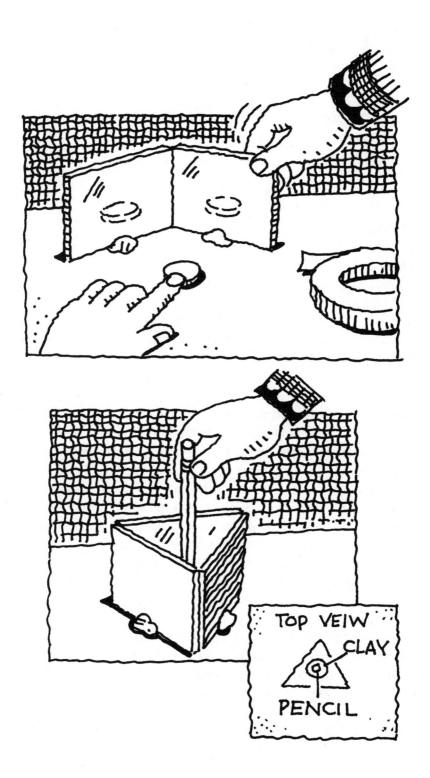

TOP VEIW

CLAY

PENCIL

1.18 KALEIDOSCOPE

A kaleidoscope is a toy that uses reflected images to produce cool patterns. Would you like to see how one works? Just follow these instructions.

Materials
* *three small plastic mirrors (with frames removed)*
* *tape*
* *wax paper*
* *pair of scissors*
* *rubber band*
* *several small and transparent colored beads*

CAUTION
If you use glass mirrors, do not remove the glass from its frame. Exposed glass edges of these mirrors are extremely sharp.

To Do
Arrange the mirrors to form a triangular viewing tube. The reflecting sides of the mirrors should face inward. Use tape to secure this shape.

Cut out a piece of wax paper that is slightly larger than the triangular open end. Cover one end with the wax paper. Pull the paper tight. Use a rubber band to secure the paper to the tube end.

Drop several small colored beads into the tube. If you don't have beads, small pieces of colored plastic or tissue paper will also work.

Look into the open end of the kaleidoscope. What do you see? How many reflections are there? Shake the tube so that the beads move to new positions. What do you see now?

The Science
The magic of the kaleidoscope arises from its creation of multiple reflections. The angle of the three mirrors, however, limits the number of reflections. Each of the reflections (and the real screen) appears attached to its neighboring reflections.

CHECK IT OUT! Why do kaleidoscopes have a part that turns?

TAPE

RUBBER BAND

WAX PAPER

MIRROR

1.19 UP PERISCOPE

What type of craft do you think of when you hear the word "periscope"? Although submarines might be the most common answer, periscopes are also found on many aircraft. The pilots can use these seeing devices to examine the landing gear and other external parts of the craft without having to step outside. Not bad, especially when you consider that the outside environment might have a breeze of 400 mph and a temperature of 50° below zero!

Materials
* two plastic mirrors
* tape
* pair of scissors
* empty spaghetti box (1 pound size)

CAUTION
If you use glass mirrors, do not remove the glass from its frame. Exposed glass edges of these mirrors are extremely sharp.

To Do
Cut off the flaps at both ends of the spaghetti box. You'll need to make two observation windows. The windows will be at the opposite sides and ends of the box.

To make each observation window, you'll need to remove a rectangular section of the box. The section begins at the edge of the box and extends 2 inches.

Next, you'll need to make mirror slots. The slots will be made on the box sides that have not been cut. They are cut at 45° angles as shown in the illustration. Each of the four slots should be wide enough to fit a mirror.

Insert the mirrors across the slots. Secure the mirrors with tape. You may wish to cover the open ends of the box with masking tape.

Look through one of the windows and what do you see? If nothing appears, you'll need to adjust the placement of the mirrors.

The Science

The illustration should explain it all!

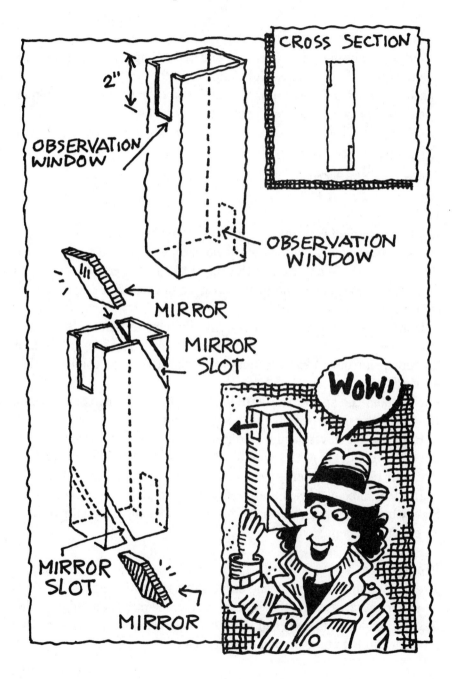

CROSS SECTION

2"

OBSERVATION WINDOW

OBSERVATION WINDOW

MIRROR

MIRROR SLOT

MIRROR SLOT

MIRROR

WOW!

1.20 REFLECTIONS IN A SPOON

Funhouse mirrors can reflect some pretty strange images. Look into one mirror and your body might appear 10 feet tall. Walk in front of another mirror and you might look as if you didn't have a midsection. These kinds of distortion are produced by curves.

Materials
* shiny metal tablespoon

To Do
Hold up a shiny metal tablespoon. Note that the bowl-like part of the spoon has two sides. The side of the bowl that bulges outward is called the convex side. When we use the spoon to eat, the convex side faces downward. The side of the bowl that goes inward (forming a depression) is called the concave side.

Hold the spoon vertically. Look into the convex side of the spoon. How does your image appear? Is your image right-side up or is it flipped upside down? Is your image stretched? If so, do you look taller or wider?

Now hold the spoon horizontally. Look into the convex side again. How does the distortion change as you turn the spoon?

Hold the spoon vertically. Flip it around so that you are looking at the concave side. How does your image look now? Is it right-side up? Are your features distorted?

Hold the spoon horizontally. How does it affect the image now? Slowly bring the spoon closer to your face. Does the image flip or does it remain the same?

The Science
The distortion is caused by the curved surface of the mirror. As side-by-side light rays strike the curves, they are sent back at slightly different angles. It's this spreading or concentrating of rays that causes the reflections to take on odd appearances.

1.21 IT'S A WRAP

Several years ago, all wrapping paper used to be made of paper. Nowadays, you can get wrapping material that is made of very thin plastic. Some of this plastic material has a reflective silver covering. Perhaps you've received a birthday gift wrapped in this reflective material? If so, what did you do with the mirrored fabric after you ripped it off your present? Hopefully, you kept it around for this next experiment.

Materials
* silver-coated wrapping material
* glue stick
* index card
* pair of scissors

To Do
Cut out a card-sized rectangle of silver-coated wrapping material. Use a glue stick to coat an index card with a thin and uniform layer of adhesive. Place the sliver rectangle in the center of the card. Gently press it from the center of the card. Try to squeeze out any bubbles or regions where the material forms a bump or fold. Let dry.

Examine the silver-coated card. Can you see your reflection in the card? Does this material make a good mirror?

While looking at your reflection, bend the card. Make the card into a convex mirror by having the center bend towards you. Make the bend up and down. Make the bend sideways. What happens to the distortion as you change the angle of this bend?

Now bend the card into a concave mirror. Can you locate the viewing distance where your image flips upside down?

The Science
A good mirror has a reflective surface that's both silver-coated and extremely flat. Glass that is coated with silver paint makes a great mirror. The wrapping paper, however, wasn't so perfect. Although the material was coated in silver, it wasn't very flat. Slight bumps in its surface produced major distortions that spoiled its reflecting possibilities.

1.22 ONE WAY OUT

What a strange place for a mirror! Why would someone want to place a mirror behind that check-out counter? There's no accounting for the manager's sense of decor, unless of course she's on the lookout for shoplifters.

Material
* *silver packaging wrap*

To Do
Turn up the lights in the room you're in. Stretch the reflective sheet of silver wrap so that it is taut. Hold it at arm's length and examine your reflection. Weird.

Now bring the material close to your face so that it touches your nose. Can you see any objects in the room?

Call for a friend's attention. While holding up the material, make faces. Have your friend try to figure out what you are doing. Although he or she won't be able to see in, you'll be able to see out. Their image will be dim, but it will be visible!

The Science
This wrapping material makes a great one-way mirror. This property is produced by a thin silvery coating. Like the one-way mirrored glass (used in stores), this material had a covering that wasn't thick enough to block all light. It allowed some light through.

To increase the one-way experience, objects on one side of the glass are brightly lit while the objects on the other side have less illumination.

1.23 CD COPIER

Walk by the large glass window of a store. Look into the display and most likely you'll see someone familiar staring right back out. Although glass is transparent, it has some reflective qualities. In this experiment, you'll use both properties of glass to construct a cool copying machine.

Materials
* clear plastic CD case
* pen
* blank sheet of paper
* lamp (if available)

To Do
Place a blank sheet of paper alongside an image you wish to trace. Remove the cardboard insert from a clear CD case. Open and position the case so that the clear plastic section is aligned along the border of the two papers.

Look into the plastic. Do you see a ghost-like reflection? You can increase the intensity of this reflected image by shining a bright light on the original copy while dimming the light over the blank copy sheet. By following the image outline, you can trace a copy of the original onto the blank paper. How is this copy similar to the original? How is it different?

The Science
The clear plastic case has some reflective qualities. Light from the original drawing traveled to the plastic case. Some of it was reflected off the surface and back to your eyes.

When you looked through the plastic case, you were able to "project" this reflected image onto the blank sheet of paper. The drawing that you created was right/left reversed, since it was a copy of a reflected mirror image.

1.24 MIRROR MAGIC

Smoke and mirrors. For centuries, this phrase was the magician's hallmark. It was believed that most stage illusions were accomplished with the aid of these tools. One of the more popular tricks of the 1800s was making your assistant disappear and reappear at will. Although we won't tell you how it was done, you might figure it out after performing this experiment.

Materials
* clear drinking glass
* plastic CD case
* candle
* matches
* plate

NOTE: Since this experiment requires the use of an open flame, it must be performed with adult supervision. Before lighting any matches, make sure that all long hair and loose clothing are tied back.

To Do
Remove the cardboard insert from a clear CD case. Open and position the case so that the clear plastic sections form a stable right angle.

Place a drinking glass on the near side of the clear plastic. Place a candle on a plate and position them on the opposite side of the CD case.

Have an adult light the candle. From the drinking glass side, look into the plastic and find the reflection of the glass.

Move the glass so that its reflection aligns with the lit candle. Dim the lights in the room. When the glass is in the correct position, the reflection and transmitted image will combine to make it appear as if the candle is burning within the glass. Magic? Heck no—it's science!

The Science
The image that you see in the CD case is a mix of both reflected light and transmitted light. The reflected light comes from the drinking glass. The transmitted light comes from the candle. Since both images overlap, your brain assumes that they came from the same location and places the burning candle in the glass.

1.25 REAPPEARING ACT

For our next trick, we are going to make one billion dollars appear from nowhere! Applause. Sorry, we are mistaken. Due to tax laws, we won't be able to work with such a large sum of money. We will, however, make a hidden penny magically reappear. Less applause.

Materials
* opaque soup bowl or mug
* water-filled cup
* penny

To Do
Place a penny in the bottom of an opaque soup bowl or mug. Position yourself off to the side. Slowly lower your viewing angle until the penny can no longer be seen. What happened to the coin? Did it disappear?

Suppose light rays didn't travel in straight lines. How might a curved ray affect your observations? While keeping your viewing angle, slowly add water from the cup into the bowl.

As the level of water rises, you may be surprised to observe your "lost" penny. What caused the coin to reappear?

The Science
Although light rays travel straight paths, these paths change direction as light moves from one substance to another. The border (scientists often call this an interface) between the water's surface and the surrounding air causes light rays to bend. So when you look at the water's surface, you don't see objects that are in a direct line-of-sight. Instead, you see things that are submerged and out of a direct line-of-sight.

1.26 MORE MAGIC

(O)kay. Okay. Okay. You liked the last trick. Applause. Now you want another magic trick to play on your little brother or sister. How about a disappearing act? No, we won't make him or her disappear. Less applause. Instead, you'll focus your art of illusion on a less pestering subject—another penny.

Materials
* two clear drinking glasses
* saucer
* water
* penny

To Do
Be theatrical. Have your audience focus their attention on your magical skills, props, and presentation. Place the base of a clear drinking glass over a penny.

Cover the mouth of the glass with a small saucer (the saucer prevents people from seeing straight down into the glass). From the side, your audience members will observe the penny. Make sure that everyone can see the penny.

Now tilt back the saucer and fill the glass with water. Again, cover up the mouth of the glass with the saucer. Can the audience still see the penny? What happened to it?

The Science
It's those bending light rays again. The image of the coin travels along straight-line paths. When the glass is empty (actually it's filled with air), there is little distortion and the rays travel a mostly straight path from the coin to your eyes. The water changes things.

Now, the light rays first travel in water. When they strike the side of the glass, some of them are bent and travel up the side of the glass. The light rays that do escape from the glass are bent so much that they travel almost straight up and are blocked by the part of the saucer that extends past the mouth of the glass. Since the rays carrying the coin's image can't get to your eyes, the object has "disappeared."

AUDIENCE

SAUCER

COIN

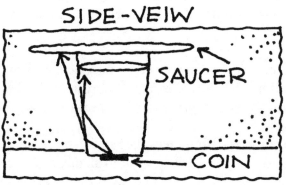

SIDE-VEIW

SAUCER

COIN

1.27 LIGHTS OUT

Wow! That guy jumped right out of the screen! How did they make those 3D effects? If you tried to remove your viewing glasses, you probably were disappointed. The movie looked out of focus. Actually, there were two movies which were projected onto the same screen. The eyeglasses contained *polarizing lenses*. These special lenses separated the overlapping movies and sent a different image to each eye. Your brain did the rest and produced the illusion of 3D.

Materials

* *two pairs of polarizing sunglasses (not just any sunglasses—the lenses must be made of polarizing material)*

NOTE: You can also use one pair of discarded polarizing glasses from which you'll remove one lens.

REMEMBER: If you borrow someone else's glasses, be kind. Don't scratch, crush, or lose them.

To Do

Close one eye. Use your open eye to look through a polarizing lens. What do you see? A slightly darkened world? Good.

Now hold up the second lens right behind the first. Look through both lenses. What do you see now?

Slowly rotate one of the lenses. What happens to your view? Can you rotate one lens so that no light passes through to your eyes?

The Science

Make a "thumbs up" sign with your hand. Good. Now extend the index finger of this hand. Your index finger represents the direction that the light ray travels. Your thumb points to the direction at which this light wave vibrates.

Rotate your wrist. Notice how the ray still travels in the same direction. However, the vibrations project in all directions along this circular path. The thumb's side-to-side waves can be cut out using polarizing filters. A polarizing filter can limit the vibrations to mostly one plane. This cuts down on the transmitted light.

When two filters are used, you can do even more. When the filters are positioned so that one knocks out up-and-down vibrations while the other cuts out side-to-side vibrations, no light is transmitted.

1.28 REVERSED WRITING

Leonardo Da Vinci wrote his journal notes backwards. People believe he did this in order to prevent others from stealing his ideas. Have you ever tried to read something that someone has written backwards? It isn't easy.

Materials
* *drawing paper*
* *carbon paper*
* *pen*
* *mirror*

To Do
Place a sheet of carbon paper face-up on the table. Place a sheet of drawing paper over the carbon paper. Sign your name. Pick up the sheet of paper and turn it around. What do you see?

Hold a mirror up to the reversed writing. What happens now?

Place this sheet of drawing paper back on the table. Hold the mirror above the paper. Look only into the reflection and write several sentences. What happens?

The Science
When you wrote your name, you pressed down on the pressure-sensitive carbon paper. The paper left an imprint of carbon on the underside of the upper sheet. When the carbon message was examined, it appeared backwards. The mirror flipped the reversed writing back to normal.

Looking at the reflection interfered with your writing. Your brain is constantly seeking feedback. Even as you write (or speak), your brain detects and analyzes the information that goes out. When the feedback appears incorrect, you brain becomes confused. It tries to correct things by changing your writing to fit the reflection.

CHECK IT OUT! Try doing a maze while looking only at its reflected image.

1.29 LENS BEND

Imagine pushing a shopping cart through a paved lot. Suddenly, the right wheels slip off the pavement and sink into sand. Although these wheels can still turn, they move much more slowly than the wheels that remain on the harder surface. The difference in speed causes the cart to turn sharply towards the sandy side.

Like the turning cart, light rays can also be redirected. Want to see?

Materials
* *ray-making tool (from "Reflected Rays" experiment, p. 32)*
* *hand lens*
* *clay*
* *flashlight*
* *clear drinking glass*
* *water*
* *a drop of milk*

To Do
Fill a glass three-fourths full with water. Set this water-filled glass on a flat surface.

Position the ray-making tool several inches from the glass. Turn on the flashlight and aim its beam through the comb's teeth. The separate rays should illuminate their path along the tabletop.

Position the glass so that these rays strike it in the center. You may have to raise the ray maker on a book to obtain the best beam angle. Observe the beams from above. What happens to rays as they strike the water-filled glass? How many times does their angle change? To help see the rays, make the water partly cloudy by adding a drop of milk.

Replace the water-filled glass with a hand lens. Position the lens so that the separate beams can be observed striking the center of the lens. What happens to these rays? Does the hand lens affect the rays in the same fashion as the water-filled glass?

The Science
As the mostly parallel light beams struck the water-filled glass, their direction changed. The first change occurred at the point where they

entered the vessel. The collision with both the glass container and water caused the light rays to bend together.

As they traveled through the water, the rays followed a straight path. When they exited the glass, their direction changed once more. Again, the rays wound up closer together. Several inches past the glass, the rays actually crossed over each other to form a bright spot. This special point is called the *focus point*. At the focus point, light rays are the most concentrated. Beyond the focus point, light rays spread out.

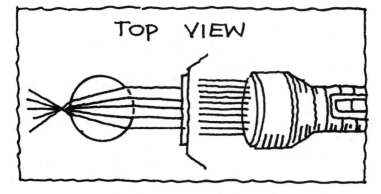

TOP VIEW

1.30 CASE OF THE WATERY MAGNIFIER

Did you know that some of the earliest magnifying lenses were built with water? Artists of ancient cultures filled round glass vessels with clear water. When these containers were placed near objects, the water magnified the objects' image. Thousands of years later, it's your turn to build a watery magnifier.

Materials
* *small, round clear plastic vial or container with cap (see note)*
* *clear water*
* *paper towel*
* *newspaper*

NOTE: There are many types and sources of these containers. The see-through hotel/personal size shampoo or body wash containers work best. You can also use small vials that hold perfume or scent samples. Even the clear plastic containers that are made for soaking contact lenses can be used. However, make sure you use only *new* containers or ones that have been thoroughly washed with soap and rinsed!

To Do
Fill the see-through container to the brim with water. Twist on the cap or snap down the lid to form a waterproof seal. Use the paper towel to wipe off any water that might be on the outside of the container.

Lay the water-filled (but dry) container on its side. Place it over a sheet of newspaper. Examine the paper's letters. What do you see? Move the container up and down. What happens to the projected image?

The Science
Within a round container, water "fills out" a curved, lens-like shape. As light rays enter and exit this watery lens, they bend. The bending of rays produces a magnified or stretched image.

1.31 THE HEAT IS ON

Close your eyes and look skyward. You can probably tell where the Sun is without looking. The warmth from its rays gives away the position of this nearby star.

Imagine what would happen if you were able to concentrate the Sun's rays. You'd produce a very bright spot. You'd also produce enough concentrated sunlight to burn through a string!

Materials
* plastic container
* tape
* nail
* black sewing thread
* hand lens
* pair of scissors

N O T E : Do this experiment with an adult!

To Do
Cut out a piece of 6-inch-long black thread. Tie one end of thread to a metal nail. Tape the other end of the thread to the neck of the container. The nail should hang freely in the center of the container.

Place the container in bright sunlight. Use a hand lens to focus a beam of light on the thread. Keep the bright spot focused on the same location. What happens? Can you explain your observations?

The Science
The hand lens focused the light rays into a very bright and hot spot. When this spot was focused on the thread, the temperature of the cotton material increased. Soon, the thread became hot enough to smoke. When enough of the fibers had burned, the thread broke and the nail fell to the bottom of the container.

1.32 BENT PENCIL

You don't have to be in the desert to see a mirage. Just look down a long road on a hot summer day. Most likely you'll see what looks like water or puddles on the road.

As you approach this slick strip of road, however, it dries up. What happened? You just experienced a mirage. This mirage was caused by the bending of light rays. What appeared as water was actually blue sky. The heated atmosphere produced a type of lens that bent the light rays. When you looked down the road, the wavy sky appeared on the ground instead of up above.

Materials
* pencil
* clear tall drinking glass
* water

To Do
Fill a drinking glass halfway with water. Place a pencil in the glass. Describe the appearance of the pencil. Is it straight or does it appear to bend or break at the spot where it enters the water?

Slowly fill the glass with water. What happens to the "break" as the water level rises?

The Science
The glass and water act as a light-bending lens. Your eyes detect the bent light rays but assume that they traveled on a straight path. Your brain "projects" where a straight path had come from. Mistakenly, it places the submerged pencil in a position where it's not.

In contrast, there is no confusion above the water's surface. This light traveled without bending. Your brain correctly projects where this part of the pencil was. The "break" arises from the two different projections.

1.33 MARBLE MAGIC

Your eye contains a part called a *lens*. Like the lens of a camera, this eye part focuses light. But unlike the camera's glass lens, yours is made of living muscle. Like other types of muscle, it can stretch and contract. By changing its shape, the lens can focus distant or close-up objects onto the light-detecting part of the eye (called the *retina*). Without the action of the lens, our visible world would be a blur.

Materials
* *white wall*
* *clear glass marble*

To Do
Stand next to a white wall. Make sure your body is well illuminated. Hold out a clear glass marble several inches from the wall's surface. Look closely at the wall just below the marble. What (or whom) do you see?

Now place the marble over a screw or scratch on the wall. Move the marble up and down until the screw is in focus. How does the marble affect the image of the screw?

The Science
The marble acts like a lens. Light rays that are reflected off your body enter the marble. They exit the marble and are cast onto the wall. If the marble is placed at the correct distance, a finely focused (and very reduced) image of your body can be seen on the wall screen.

At the same time your body shrinkage was occurring, the marble was magnifying wall objects. The screws and scratches appeared larger because the marble had spread out their reflected light rays.

1.34 PINHOLE PROJECTION

Take a look around you. Everything appears right-side up. Although this makes sense, it's not how your eye sees it. Images that are cast upon your eye's light-sensitive screen (called the *retina*) are upside down. It takes a learned brain trick to flip these images right-side up so that they match the look of the real world.

Materials

* *plastic cup*
* *wax paper*
* *pair of scissors*
* *rubber band*
* *pushpin*

To Do

Use the pushpin to punch a hole in the center of the cup's bottom. Cut out a piece of wax paper slightly larger than the cup's mouth. Stretch this paper across the mouth of the cup. Use a rubber band to secure the paper.

Darken the room. Aim the pinhole at a bright window or lamp. Look at the wax paper. What do you see? How does the image compare to the actual scene?

CAUTION
Never look directly at the Sun.

The Science

Congratulations! You've built a pinhole viewer. Light that came through the window entered into the hole of your viewer. After entering through the hole, the light rays continued on a straight path. This caused the upper light rays to strike the bottom part of the wax paper screen. Likewise, the lower light rays struck the upper part of the screen. The image that these rays produced was flipped upside down.

On the opposite page is a ray diagram that shows what happened when light from an object passed through the pinhole and was projected onto the viewing screen.

CHECK IT OUT! What eye part works like the wax paper screen?

1.35 PROJECT: PROJECTOR

The projection room at the back of a movie theater is a cool place, literally. That's because the room has an incredible network of cold air pipes. This frigid air, however, isn't meant to keep the projectionist comfortable. It is sent straight to the movie-making machines. There, it cools the projectors and movie film. Without this continual blast of frigid air, the projector and film would be ruined by the intense heat given off by the white-hot projection lamp.

Materials
* *flashlight*
* *discarded 35mm photographic slide*
* *wax paper*
* *rubber band*
* *hand lens*
* *tape*

To Do
Cover the lens of a flashlight with a double thickness of wax paper. Be careful not to crumple or wrinkle this paper. (The wax paper lens will "soften" the bright center of the beam)

Pull the wax paper tight and secure this covering with a rubber band. Place a 35mm slide on top of the wax paper. Use tape to hold the 35mm slide in place.

Turn on the flashlight. Aim the beam at a light-colored wall that is an arm's distance away. What do you see? Can you see colors? Is the image clear or fuzzy?

Place a hand lens several inches in front of the slide. Move the lens back and forth. Does the lens sharpen the projected image? Is the projected image larger or smaller than the actual drawn figure?

The Science
Congratulations! You've built a film projector. Light that was emitted by the bulb streamed through the photographic slide. From there, the light continued outward, spreading as it traveled. By the time these rays struck the wall, the beam produced an out-of-focus image. To

prevent the rays from spreading apart, a hand lens was placed into the flashlight beam. Its shape redirected the rays and focused them on the nearby wall, creating a sharp (and enlarged) image of the 35mm slide.

CHECK IT OUT! How does the projected image compare to the slide?

1.36 MONA MIA

All shadows are created equal, or are they? Hold your hand several inches above this book. Raise and lower your hand while you observe your shadow. Does the appearance of the shadow change? If so, how? When is the shadow its sharpest? When is it darkest?

Materials
* scrap paper
* carbon paper
* pair of scissors
* flashlight
* wax paper
* rubber band

To Do
Place a sheet of scrap paper beneath the weird drawing on the next page. Then, insert a sheet of carbon paper (copying side down) between the page and the scrap. Trace out the odd outline.

Use a pair of scissors to carefully cut out the carbon copy's three irregular dark shapes.

As in the previous experiment, cover the lens of a flashlight with an unwrinkled, double thickness of wax paper. Pull the wax paper tight and secure this covering with a rubber band.

Hold the cutout about 2 inches away from the wall. Aim the beam of the flashlight at the cutout. What do you see? Are the edges of the image sharp or "soft"? How many shades can you distinguish in this shadow?

Slowly move the scrap paper away from the wall. What happens to the shadow? Keep the paper stationary and continue moving the flashlight back. What happens now?

The Science
When the shadow mask is held close to the wall, a dark and sharp shadow is cast. People in science call this well-defined shadow an *umbra*. If you were the size of an ant and walked into this umbra, you wouldn't see the flashlight beam. It would be completely dark (except for the other light that was in the room).

As the shadow mask is moved away from the wall, lighter shades of shadow appear. These lighter shades form the shadow's *penumbra*.

The penumbra isn't in complete darkness. This time, our ant-sized visitor would see a part of the flashlight beam.

CHECK IT OUT! To observe the entire light beam, where would our ant have to walk?

1.37 RIGHT-SIDE DOWN?

Brain trick. Brain trick. Brain trick. You are doing it right now. Although you are totally unaware of it, your brain is flipping every-thing it sees right-side up. Without this brain flip, your world would look as topsy-turvy as the images cast upon your retina.

But suppose an image was somehow projected right-side up? Would your brain know the difference and keep the scene as it appeared? Or would it perform a flip and turn the image upside down?

Materials
* pin
* index card

To Do
Use the pin to poke a small pinhole in the center of the index card. Stand in front of a brightly lit window. Hold up the card several inch-es from your face. Look through the hole at the bright outdoors.

CAUTION
Never look directly at the Sun!

Hold the pin so that its flat head extends upwards. Position the pin head between the card's hole and your eye. First, hold the pin at a level just beneath the hole. Slowly raise the pin head. From which direction does it appear to cross the pinhole? Keep the pin head cen-tered in the hole. Describe its appearance.

NOTE: Be very careful when holding this pin or any other sharp object near your eye.

The Science
Most of the time, the light rays that cast an image cross as they stream through the eye's pupil. This produces an upside-down view that your brain has learned to flip around.

In this experiment, you've created a unique setup. The rays that come through the pinhole won't cross over themselves. They only spread out. As they stream through the pupil, they remain uncrossed and cast a right-side up image on the retina. Your brain, however, has learned to flip over everything that it sees. So even though the image is projected right-side up, your brain flips it upside down!

CHECK IT OUT! Under what conditions will a hand lens flip an image upside down?

1.38 COLOR MY WHIRL

Suppose you mixed blue and yellow pigments. You'd expect to see green.

Suppose you mixed red and white pigments. You'd expect to see pink.

But suppose you looked at a spinning disk that had a black-and-white pattern. What color or shade would you expect this blur to be?

Make a guess. Then be prepared for a surprise.

Materials
* heavy stock paper
* pair of scissors
* glue stick
* paper clip
* pushpin

To Do
Make a photocopy of the disk on the opposite page. If possible, print out this copy on heavy stock paper. If stiff paper stock is not available, you'll need to support the photocopy with a heavy stock backing. To make this backing, cut out the photocopied disk. Trace this disk onto a sheet of stiff paper. Cut out the stiff paper disk and use a glue stick to paste it to the backside of the photocopy.

Unbend one of the "arms" of a paper clip so that it looks like this:

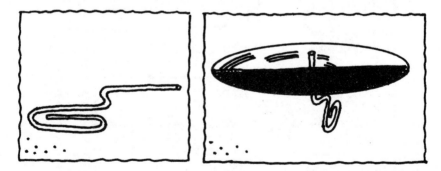

Use the pushpin to punch a hole through the center of the disk. Place the bent-up arm of the clip through this hole. The disk should rest flat and spin freely on the clip bend. Hold the disk beneath a bright light. Spin it and observe what happens to the distinct black-and-white pattern. Does this odd effect change as you vary the speed of the spin?

The Science

Colors? Where did those colors come from? No one seems to know for sure, although scientists have made some pretty good guesses.

This black-and-white pattern is called a *Benham's disk*. It was first created over 100 years ago! When it spins at the right speed, it produces a changing pattern of light that falls upon your eye's retina. Many scientists think that the pattern creates a nerve message that resembles the message for color. So when this message (which should "code" for a black-and-white spin) arrives at the brain, its content is misinterpreted. Instead, your brain thinks that this message describes a color. And so, colors where there are no colors!

1.39 CATCH A GLIMPSE

(O)verload! Overload ! Overload!

There is a limit to the amount of information that your brain can process. Think of a cartoon flipbook. When you observe a rapidly flipped sequence of drawings, it becomes impossible to distinguish individual frames. Instead, your brain gets fooled into "seeing" the illusion of continuous action.

In this experiment, you'll construct a type of strobe machine. Unlike the dance floor lights, this device doesn't depend upon flashes to create its visual trickery. Instead, the motion capture is produced by quick glimpses through rapidly spinning notches.

Materials
* pair of scissors
* pencil with eraser
* pushpin
* television screen
* kitchen sink (and faucet)
* mirror

To Do
PART 1: Hold That Pose

Make a photocopy of the disk on the opposite page. Use a pair of scissors to cut out the disk notches. Insert a pushpin through the center of the disk and anchor it to the side of a pencil's eraser. The disk should spin freely. Make sure that you assemble this spinner so that the images face away from the pencil.

First, we'll use this strobe viewer to freeze motion. Turn on a television or computer screen. Stand across the room from the screen. Shut one eye and look through any of the notches at the screen. Spin the disk. Keep looking.

As the notches rotate into view, you'll catch a quick glimpse of the screen. Does the screen's appearance change? How does increasing the spin speed affect the screen's appearance?

Adjust a cold water faucet so that a slow but steady trickle of droplets fall into the sink. Observe this motion through the notches of the spinning disk. Can you freeze the droplets in midair?

If you are having trouble seeing the droplets, try this. Fill a large paper cup with water. Add several drops of dark food coloring. Over a

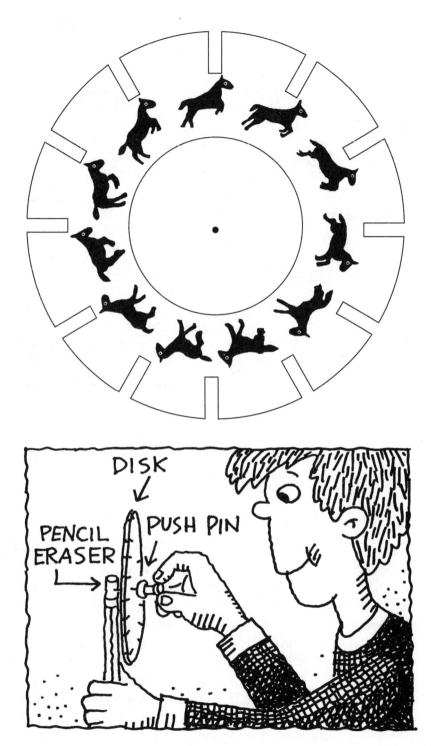

sink, have a friend use a pushpin to punch a hole in the bottom of the cup. Use your spinning disk to observe this stream of colored droplets.

PART 2: Movie Magic
Stand in front of a mirror. Look through one of the notches. Observe the reflected pattern of horses. Spin the disk. Keep looking through the notches. What do you see?

The Science
Motion that you observe on a TV screen (or movie theater or flipbook) is an illusion. It is created by a series of rapidly changing frames. Onscreen, these electronic images get "redrawn" 30 times per second. At this rate, your brain can't distinguish individual frames. In its confusion, your brain produces the illusion of smooth motion.

This strobe viewer can capture a quick glimpse of partially refreshed screens. The black bands that you observe are part of a series of incomplete screens, all captured at the same stage of refreshing.

Like the "refreshing screen," the falling droplets can also appear frozen. To produce the freeze, each quick glimpse must catch the next droplet in the same position as the previous one. This produces the illusion of a single droplet that remains in midair. To make the droplet appear to go up, each glimpse must catch the next droplet at a slightly higher position than the previous one.

Your strobe device can also be used to produce the illusion of animation. As the disk spins in front of a mirror, it offers a quick glimpse of the reflected horse images. At a fast enough speed, your brain can't distinguish the individual drawings. Instead, it blends the sequence of rapidly changing images into the illusion of smooth, animated motion.

CHECK IT OUT! What happens if the disk is spun in the opposite direction?

SOUND

2.1 BEAT BOPPERS

Have you ever gone to the movies and FELT an on-screen explosion? If so, you know that sound can be a *moving experience*. Do you remember which sounds shook you the most? Was it the high pitched whirls or the booming low pitches? While you are remembering, here's a smaller-scale rumbling (but one that's easy to observe).

Materials
* * sound system
* * foil pie pan
* * puffed cereal grains

To Do
Gently lay a speaker cabinet on its back so that its speaker faces upwards. Balance a foil pie plate on top of the speaker grill. Be careful not to push in the grill.

Pour about fifty grains of puffed cereal onto the pie plate. Make sure that the sound system is "off," with the volume turned down. Switch on the system. Slowly crank up the volume and watch what happens to the cereal!

The Science
Sound is a form of energy. It consists of vibrations that are passed from particle to particle. In air, the vibrations of sound are transferred by particles of gas that are too small to see.

The sound produced by the speaker caused air particles to vibrate. The energy of the vibration spread out and struck the bottom of the pan. The large (and light) bottom of the pan was struck by a good deal of sound energy. This energy caused the pan to vibrate. The energy of vibration was then transferred to the cereal grains. As they became energized, the puffs jumped to the beat.

CHECK IT OUT! How do pitch and loudness affect the bouncing grains?

2.2 SQUISH IN MOTION

Fill a bathroom sink halfway with water. Stick your index finger in the water. Once it's wet, position this finger about 1 foot above the water's surface. Let the drips fall into the water below. What happens at the spot where the drop strikes the water? Describe any changes in the water's surface.

Materials
* *metal coil toy*
* *tape*

To Do
Place the coil toy on a section of floor that is not covered by a rug or carpet. Use tape to secure one end of the coil to a wall.

Stretch out the coil spring several feet. Hold the free end of the coil in one hand. With your other hand, strike this end with a swift hit. What happens to the coil? Can you detect a wave? What is the wave made of? Which way does it move? Does it bounce off the wall? If so, in which direction does the reflected wave travel?

The Science
Sound travels in waves. Its waves are formed by regions of matter that are squished together. When you struck the metal coil, you squished together some of the windings. It was this "squish" that moved along the coil. If your slap was strong enough, the "squish" had enough energy to strike the wall and reflect back down the coil. When a sound is created, air particles get squished together. This compressed region of air transfers its energy to the neighboring particles, and the squish (not the air particles) carries the sound along.

By the way, scientists prefer the term *compressional wave*, but it's the same thing as the squished wave we've been talking about.

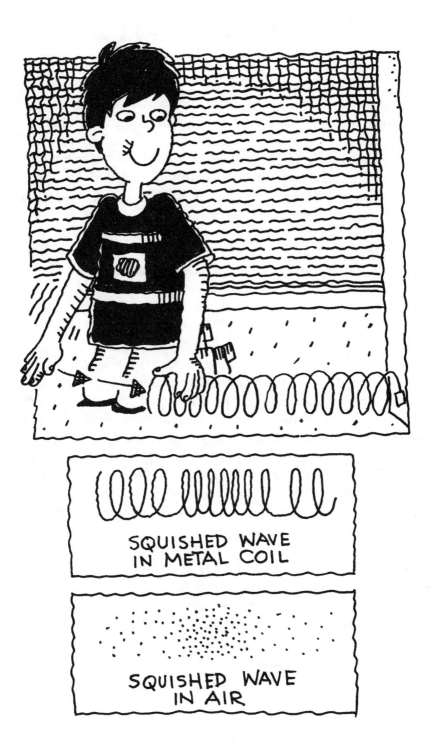

SQUISHED WAVE
IN METAL COIL

SQUISHED WAVE
IN AIR

2.3 SOUND FILM

Have you ever removed the front cloth or grill covering of a speaker cabinet? If so, you exposed the sound-pushing surface of the speaker. Turn up the stereo and the speakers vibrate back and forth. The louder the sound, the greater the movement. In this experiment, you'll construct a device that will also move with the music. Unlike the plastic or cardboard speaker cone, your device will be made from something slightly more fragile—soap bubble film!

Materials
* *paper drinking cup*
* *bubble solution*
* *speaker*
* *pair of scissors*
* *shallow plate*

To Do
Use your scissors to cut off a "collar" from the cup's rim. The collar should be about 1 inch wide and form a continuous round band.

Pour some bubble solution in a shallow plate. Set the "lip" side of the collar into the solution. Turn on a nearby sound system. Make sure that the sound isn't too loud, or else you may damage your hearing.

Carefully raise the collar so that a film forms across the rim opening. While holding the outside of the rim, position the film in front of the speaker. What happens to the bubble film? How might changes in the volume affect the film? Do you think low pitches or high pitches will cause more movement? Why?

The Science
Bubble film is a very thin surface made from water and soap particles. Since it is lean and light, it requires very little energy to get it moving. As the speaker cone moved in and out, it vibrated surrounding air particles. An energy wave was formed. As this wave moved outward, it struck the bubble film, causing it to vibrate in a pattern that copied the sound's intensity.

2.4 SEEING WITH SOUND

Crash! A sudden sound jolts you from your sleep. What was it? Monsters? Aliens? Distant cousins? As your mind races, your hearing switches to its super-detection mode. Yes, you hear footsteps moving in the hall. By the speed and volume of the footsteps, you realize that it's only your little brother. Whew!

Materials
* *small pizza box*
* *scrap cardboard*
* *marble*
* *pair of scissors*
* *tape*
* *a friend*

To Do
Trim several scraps of cardboard into strips that are about 1 inch wide. Open the pizza box.

Fold and position these strips into a simple shape such as a circle, triangle, or square. Secure the cardboard shape with tape to the bottom of the open box. Make sure that the lid can be closed over the cardboard shape.

Insert a marble between the shape and the box edge. Seal the box shut and give it to a friend. Challenge your friend to uncover the shape by "listening" to the roll of the marble.

Now switch roles by having your friend construct a different shape for you to uncover.

The Science
The sounds detected by your ears are changed into nerve messages and sent to your brain. As your brain processes this information, it figures out all sorts of things about the sound. By analyzing changes in speed and volume, you can figure out the angles at which the marble rolls.

Of course, you can also "cheat" by feeling the collisions of the marble with the cardboard. When your brain combines all of this information, it constructs the most likely shape encountered by the rolling marble.

2.5 SOUND SPOTS

Place your palm about 1 foot in front of your mouth. Count from one to ten. As you count, slowly bring your palm closer to your mouth. Most likely, by the time you reach "five" you'll feel the sound waves as they strike your hand. Now keep you palm about 6 inches from your mouth. Again, count from one to ten. Can you "feel" the difference in the sounds of each number?

Materials
* cardboard tube (from a finished roll of toilet paper)
* wax paper
* rubber band
* sequin or mirrored plastic chip
* glue
* pair of scissors
* flashlight

To Do
Cut out a 4-inch-square wax paper. Stretch the paper over one end of the cardboard tube. Pull it tight to form a flat surface. Slip a rubber band over the wax paper to keep it in place.

Use glue to secure a sequin to the center of the wax paper. Hold the open end of the tube to your mouth. Use your other hand to aim a flashlight beam at the sequin. Stand near a wall so that you can locate the reflected spot of light. Talk loudly into the tube. Observe how your voice affects the spot.

The Science
As you spoke, you produced sound waves. These waves (which consist of pushed-together particles of air) moved outward from your mouth and traveled into the tube. At the far end of the tube, the waves struck the wax paper. This collision caused the stretched paper to vibrate. As the paper moved, the spot of light reflected by the sequin traced out the vibration pattern.

2.6 WHAT DOES IT MATTER?

What does it matter? Plenty. In order to produce sound, you need something to vibrate. Matter is that something. It's the "stuff" that the universe is made of. But will all matter transmit sound? Are there only certain particles that can pass these sound waves along? Let's find out.

Materials
* three plastic sealable bags
* sand (sugar or flour can be substituted)
* water
* coin

To Do
Fill the first bag halfway with sand. Push out the extra air and seal the bag shut. Fill a second bag halfway with water. Again, push out the extra air and seal the bag shut. Make sure that it doesn't leak. Fill a third bag halfway with air. Seal it and place all three bags on a table-top.

Place your ear on the bag of sand. Gently tap a coin on the tabletop. What do you hear? Repeat the coin taping while listening through the bag of water. Does it sound the same? How has the taping sound changed? Repeat the tapping one more time while listening through the bag filled with air. Compare the three sounds.

The Science
Sounds are transferred by particles that slam into neighboring particles. Solids contain particles with the closest neighbors. Next comes liquids. Gases have the most spread-out particles.

The closer the particles are to each other, the better the sound transmission. That's why the sound that passed through the solid and liquid may have seemed much louder than the sound that passed through the air-filled bag.

2.7 SURFACE SOUND

Let's be critical. Fill a plastic bag full of water. Seal the bag and listen through it by placing your ear against its surface. Which type of matter did the sound have to travel through in order to reach your ear?

a) solid; b) liquid; c) gas

If you answered "liquid," you're only partially correct. The sound was also carried by the solid plastic covering.

Materials
* *wristwatch (old wind-up type)*
* *large plastic sealable bag*

To Do
Wind up the wristwatch. Make sure that it works. Place the watch on a flat surface. Position your ear about 6 inches above the watch. Can you hear it tick?

Fill a plastic bag with air and seal it shut. Place the bag over the watch. Place your ear on the surface of the bag. Can you hear the ticking now? Why?

The Science
Without the bag, the ticking sound was transferred only by air. Since air particles are very spread out, this type of transfer is not effective.

When the bag full of air was used, things changed. The ticks were absorbed by the plastic skin of the bag. The sound energy was then transferred by the plastic particles along the surface of the bag. Since the particles of this solid were concentrated, less sound energy was lost. This produced a volume that was loud enough to detect.

But don't forget, the total sound also depended upon what was in the bag. In this case, it was air.

2.8 IT RULES

"Don't do that!"

"The ruler isn't meant to be snapped like that."

"You'll break it in half and then how will you measure things?"

Okay, it's time to break rules (but not the ruler). In this experiment, you'll get to do something you may have been told not to do—twang a ruler off the edge of a desk. By investigating this twang, you'll have fun while uncovering a sound relationship.

Materials
* ruler (wooden or plastic)
* a sturdy desk

To Do
Position a ruler so that half of it extends beyond the desk edge. Use one hand to press down on the ruler, keeping it firmly against the desktop. Use your other hand to bend up the free end of the ruler. Don't pull too much or else you might snap the ruler (and be treated to a chorus of "I told you so"). Release the bent end and listen to the sound.

Now slide the ruler back so that less of it extends beyond the desktop. Repeat the bend and release. What happened to the sound of the twang?

Retract it farther. What happens to the sound as less of the ruler is extended beyond the desk?

Slide the ruler in the opposite direction. What happens to the sound when more of the ruler extends over the desk edge?

The Science
As you guessed, the vibrating ruler produces the twang sound. It's the portion of the ruler that extends beyond the desk that makes the sound. The part that is pressed firmly against the desk cannot vibrate. Therefore, this section doesn't make any sound. As less of the ruler was extended beyond the edge, a higher-pitched sound was created. The more it extended, the lower the pitch.

2.9 PLANTED SOUNDS

Have you ever looked closely at a saxophone or clarinet mouthpiece? If so, you probably observed that the mouthpiece contains a thin piece of wood. This part of the instrument is called a *reed*. When you blow across the reed, you set it vibrating. It's this back-and-forth movement that produces the instrument's sound. As these vibrations travel through the instrument's body, the sound is "shaped" into a pleasing note.

Materials
* *blade of grass*
* *paper*
* *pair of scissors*
* *clear plastic wrapping*

To Do
Hold out your hands. Place your thumbs side-by-side together. You should observe a slender gap between them. This opening begins at the middle joint and stretches downward to the base of the thumbs.

Now position a blade of grass in this passageway. The top of the blade should be held in place between the two middle joints. The bottom of the blade should be secure between the two thumb bases.

Blow through the passageway. What do you hear?

If no sound is produced, make sure that the blade lies in the middle of the gap. Try replacing the grass blade with a blade-sized scrap of paper (you may have to wet the paper). You can also cut a similar shape of thin, light-gauge plastic.

Practice with various materials and observe the difference in the quality of the sounds.

The Science
As air rushed through the slender opening, it caused the blade to vibrate. This vibration shaped the passing air into sound waves.

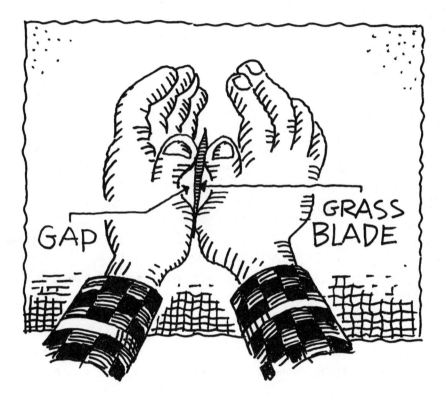

2.10 STRAW SOUNDS

The reeds of woodwind instruments are often taken from special cane plants that grow only in a region of France. Musicians believe that these plants offer the best natural material for producing the vibrating sound-maker of a woodwind instrument. Can other materials be used? You be the judge.

Materials
* drinking straw
* pair of scissors

To Do
Chew down the end of a straw so that it's crushed flat. Take a pair of scissors and carefully snip away the corners of the flattened end. The snips should produce a reed that looks like a flattened triangle (as shown in the picture).

Make sure that the reed end of the straw didn't seal itself. If it is closed, just run the end through your teeth so that it "pops" back open.

Here's the part that may take some practice. Place the reed end of the straw in your mouth. Make sure that it doesn't touch the inside of your cheek or tongue. Blow through the straw. When the cut ends vibrate, they act like the reed of a saxophone or clarinet.

Patience, patience, patience. You may not produce any sound on your first try. If nothing comes out, make sure that the reed end is still open. Try again and make sure that the reed is free to vibrate. Next, try chewing down on the reed to "soften" it up. If you still can't get a sound, snip off the end and remake the reed.

The Science
As you blew air through the straw, the air moved along the plastic reed. This force caused the reed's cut ends to vibrate. These flaps produced a vibration in the air that moved through the straw. Your ears detected this vibration as a buzzing note with a steady pitch.

2.11 CUT THAT NOTE

Imagine being able to see a column of vibrating air. In the instrument you just created in the last experiment, this vibration would stretch from one end of the straw to the other. If you were to stretch the straw, the vibrating column would also stretch. Likewise, if you were to cut off sections of the straw, the column would also shorten. So why should you care? Listen.

Materials
* *drinking straw*
* *pair of scissors*

To Do
Follow the steps in the last experiment to construct a straw instrument. Once you have mastered the playing technique, pick up a pair of scissors.

Blow through the tube to produce a loud and steady note. Carefully, use your scissors to snip off a 1-inch segment from the far end of the straw. What happens to the note?

Snip off another 1-inch section. What happens now?

If there's still enough straw left, snip off one more section. How does the sound change?

The Science
Each time you removed a section of the straw, you shortened the tube length. Since the tube was shorter, the column of vibrating air was also shortened.

When you snipped away straw sections, the note rose in pitch (also known as *frequency*). As you heard, the shortest column produced the highest-pitch sound.

Real World Connection
Have you ever seen a large pipe organ? If so, you probably observed two of its main parts: a keyboard and a series of pipes. Some of these pipes can be a tall as a small building. When air travels through these giant pipes, it produces a long column of vibrating air. This long col-

umn produces the low (or bass) notes of the pipe organ. In contrast, when air travels through the instrument's shortest pipes, it produces notes of higher pitch.

2.12 ESCAPE HATCH

Penny whistles are instruments with built in mouthpieces. When the musician blows into the mouthpiece, air is set in motion. This back-and-forth movement produces a steady pitch. When the musician wants to change the pitch, he or she covers or opens holes in the instrument's tube.

Materials
* *drinking straws*
* *pair of scissors*

To Do
Follow the steps in "Straw Sounds" experiment (p. 108) to construct a straw instrument. Make two snips with your scissors to carefully place a small opening midway in the straw. This opening will offer a short-cut for air to escape without traveling the entire distance of the instrument tube. When making the snips, make sure that your cuts do not go through the straw and divide the tube in half.

Cover the hole with your fingertip. Blow through the tube to produce a loud and steady note. Uncover the hole. What happens to the pitch? Cover the hole again. What happens now?

Place a series of holes along the length of the straw. Now try covering different combinations. How can you produce different notes? How does the position of the hole affect the instrument's sound?

BAGPIPE BLUES: A *drone* is a note that keeps playing as other notes change. You can produce the drone sound of a bagpipe by playing two straws at once. Place a note hole in one straw. Put both straws in your mouth and blow. Open and close the hole and you'll produce a changing note that harmonizes with the drone note.

The Science
When all of the instrument's holes were closed, the vibrating wave occupied the entire length of the instrument tube. This produced the instrument's lowest pitch. When a hole "opened," air escaped through

this shortcut. Since the sound wave was shortened, the note became higher in pitch.

2.13 SLIPPING AND SLIDING

Do you like to slide into things? If so, this next experiment may be ideal for you.

Materials

* straw
* pair of scissors
* plastic cup
* water

To Do

Use your scissors to cut partly through a straw. The snip should cut almost all the way through the straw but leave a solid piece so that the straw doesn't break into two separate segments. This cut should be made at about 2 inches from one end of the straw.

Carefully bend the straw so that the cut opens into a right angle as shown in the illustration. You may need to trim some excess material to ease the bend.

Fill a cup three-fourths full of water. Place the longer end of the bent straw into the cup. Place your lips on the free end and gently blow into the straw. What do you hear? If no whistling sound is produced, try pinching the top of the open straw.

Once a steady note is made, raise and lower the straw in the water. What happens to the sound?

The Science

As you blew into the short segment of straw, you created a tiny jet of air. As this jet rushed across the opening of the longer segment, it set the air within the lower section in motion. The vibration of this air column produced a slight but steady whistle.

When the straw was placed deeper into the cup, water rose and filled more of the air space. This shortened the column of vibrating air to produce a higher pitch. When the cup was lowered, the level of water within the straw dropped. This lengthened the column of vibrating air to produce a lower pitch.

2.14 PLUCKER UP

$\mathcal{S}$trike a small bell with a mallet. The vibrating bell produces a tiny "tink" sound, possibly too soft to detect. Crack the same mallet on a larger bell and you'll create a loud "gong" sound. This bigger sound results from the bell's larger shape. Since the large bell traps a greater volume of air, it produces many more air vibrations. These extra vibrations add sound richness and pump up the volume!

Materials
* kite string
* paper cup
* paper clip
* pushpin
* pair of scissors
* tape

To Do
Cut a ½-foot segment of kite string. Position the string between the thumb and index fingers of both hands. Pull your hands apart so that the string is taut. This next part may take some practice.

Turn one hand so that one (any one) finger can pluck the taut string. What do you hear? Describe the sound.

Use the pushpin to punch a small hole near the center of the bottom of a paper cup. Pass the string through the hole so that it is positioned halfway through the cup.

Tie a paper clip to the string's end that extends from the inside of the cup. Pull back on the other end of the string so that the paper clip is pulled against the inner surface of the cup bottom.

Cover your ear with the opening of the cup. Pull on the string so that it is taut.

Pluck the string. Describe the sound. How does this sound compare with the earlier sound?

The Science
When the string was first plucked, it vibrated and energized any air particles that were in direct contact with the moving material. Since relatively few particles were energized, the sound was very soft.

When the cup was added to the system, things changed. The string's vibrations were easily transferred to the cup. The larger volume of trapped air also vibrated to produce a much richer and louder sound. In addition, some of the sound was now transmitted along a solid path from the vibrating cup to the skin's surface to the middle ear.

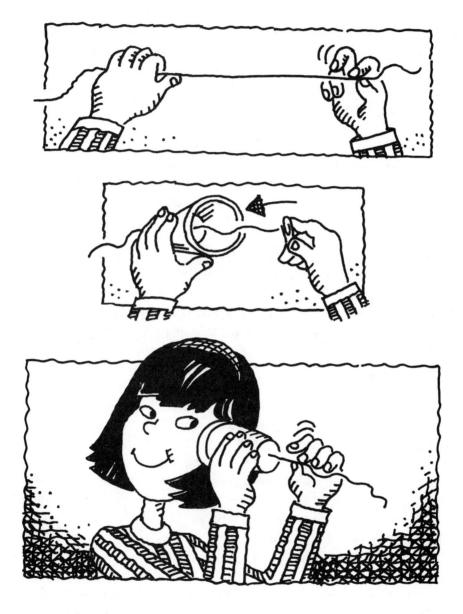

2.15 PARTY LINE

Imagine five dominos positioned one right after the next. Push over the first domino and what happens? The first domino falls into the second. The second falls into the third. The third falls into the fourth...

Imagine the tiny particles (atoms and molecules) that make up a kite string. In a similar way, motion can be transferred from particle to particle. Although you can't see this transfer, you can observe its effect using a string telephone.

Materials
* three paper cups
* kite string
* three paper clips
* pair of scissors
* pushpin
* some friends

To Do
Use a pushpin to punch a hole in the bottom of each paper cup. Cut a segment of kite string about 20 feet long.

Pass one end of the string through the bottom hole of one cup. Tie a paper clip to the end of the string that projects from the inner side of the cup. Pull on the string so that the paper clip lies flat against the inside bottom of the cup.

Place a second cup and paper clip on the other end of this string.

Move the two cups apart so that the line between them is pulled taut. Have a friend whisper into one cup. Place the other cup over your ear. Can you hear what your friend is saying? Reverse the roles. Can your friend detect your whispers?

Now cut a 10-foot segment of kite string. Place a cup and paper clip at one end of this line. Tie the free end to the middle of the two-cup line. Does this three-party line also transmit sound? How many more extensions can you add? Make a guess and then invite some friends to build a large string network.

The Science
As one person spoke into the microphone cup, the movement of air struck the cup's solid bottom, causing it to vibrate. This energy of vibration was transferred into the string. Like falling dominos, the

atoms of the strings passed the vibrations from atom to atom. Eventually, the string vibrations reached the listening cups. At these cups, the string movements were transferred to the cup bottoms. The vibrating bottoms set the air within the cup in motion. As this vibrating air struck your eardrum, you detected it as sound.

CHECK IT OUT! Do you think that metal wire makes a better or worse conductor of sound? Give it a try.

2.16 KING GONG

What can you do with a hanger? Without too much thought you can hang clothes on it. If you're good at twisting the wire, you can make all sorts of sculptures and wire tools. But did you know that you can build an incredible sound-making device from a hanger? Here's how.

Materials
* metal clothes hanger
* kite string
* metal spoon
* two paper clips
* two paper cups
* pair of scissors
* pushpin

To Do
Use a pushpin to punch a hole into the bottom of a paper cup. Cut two segments of kite string, each about 2 feet long. Pass one of the segments through the cup hole. Tie the end of this string segment that exits the inner side of the cup to a paper clip.

Repeat the above steps with another cup. When you're finished, you should have two listening devices that look as if they were cut from a string telephone.

Tie the free end of both strings to the hook of a metal hanger. Place each cup over your outer ear. Make sure that the hanger dangles freely.

Have a friend gently tap the hanger with a metal spoon or similar object. What do you hear?

The Science
Sound travels very well through solid materials. When the hanger was struck by the spoon, it vibrated. These vibrations were transferred to the string. The string carried these back-and-forth movements to the cups. There, the vibrating cup bottoms set the air space in motion.

As particles of air vibrated within the cup, they struck your eardrum. You detected this movement as sound. Since the sound traveled along the solid string, it contained much of its original energy and produced a noise that sounded like the ringing of a huge bell.

CHECK IT OUT! How might a plastic-coated hanger affect the sound? Make your prediction and then give it a try.

2.17 CACKLING CUP

Cock-a-doodle-do. It's time to wake up and build a device that sounds like a screaming rooster. Not only is the cackling cup fun to construct, but it also demonstrates how a bell shape can increase the loudness of sounds. So listen up and get to work.

Materials
* *paper cup (opaque cold drink style)*
* *kite string*
* *paper clip*
* *pair of scissors*
* *pushpin*
* *sponge or sheet of paper towel*

To Do
Use the pushpin to create a hole in the center of the cup's bottom. Cut a section of kite string about 2 feet long.

Tie a paper clip to one end of the string. Wet the free end of the string and pass it through the hole in the cup. Make sure that the paper clip winds up on the outer side of the cup.

Moisten a sponge or a sheet of paper towel.

Hold the cup so that the string is falling freely from the cup. Firmly grasp the string with the sponge. Gently tug on the string so that the sponge slips downward. What do you hear each time the sponge moves?

If no sound is produced, wet the sponge again. Squeeze out any excess water and repeat. Practice your tugging technique until you can produce the sound of a rooster's call.

The Science
As the sponge was tugged down the string, it produced vibrations. These vibrations traveled up the string and were transferred to the cup. Air that was trapped within the cup was set in motion. The cup's shape helped amplify this motion so that a loud sound was produced by this cackling cup.

CHECK IT OUT! How do you think that the size of the cup affects the sound? Make a prediction. Then test your guess.

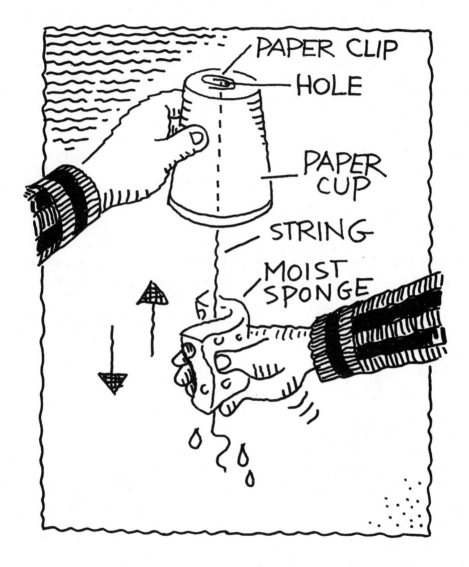

2.18 SINGING BALLOON

Place your hand gently over your throat. Hum a tune. What do you feel? Can you detect any changes in the vibration as you vary the pitch and volume of the notes? Within your throat is a body part called a voice box. The voice box contains bands of muscle tissue called *vocal cords*. Like other muscles, the vocal cords can relax or tighten up. As air passes over these muscles, their tension "shapes" the sound that you create.

Materials
* *balloon*

To Do
Blow up a balloon and hold the open end shut.

While preventing air from escaping, pinch both sides of this nozzle. Now slowly loosen your hold of the balloon's opening to allow a controlled flow of air through. Then pull the opening wider. What happens to the pitch?

Release the "stretch" so that the nozzle material relaxes. How does this affect the pitch?

The Science
The nozzle was a model of your vocal cords. Air that passed through the nozzle opening caused the elastic material to vibrate. This vibration produced sound.

When the nozzle was stretched, the vibrating material became tighter. This change produced a note of higher pitch.

When the nozzle material was relaxed, the pitch dropped. By altering the tension in the nozzle, you produced a sliding scale of notes.

2.19 KAZOO KAZOO?

Kazoos are great fun, especially for those who don't have a great singing voice. Just hum into the mouthpiece and the vibrating drum enriches your sound with a chorus of buzzing plastic. Although you can purchase kazoos at local toy stores, here's one that you can construct at home.

Materials
* clean cardboard tube (removed from paper toweling)
* pair of scissors
* cellophane-type plastic
* tape

To Do
Find a scrap piece of cellophane-type plastic. This clear, light-gauge plastic is easily recognized by the "crinkling sound" it makes when crumpled.

Cut off a section of cardboard tube that is about 6 inches long. Squish down this tube.

Use your scissors to carefully cut a rectangle about the size of a postage stamp near the middle of the tube. Cover the hole with cellophane. Use tape to secure all four edges of the plastic to the tube.

Hum into one end of the tube. What do you hear? How is the sound produced? Can you change the characteristics of the sound by using different-sized holes? Try it and find out!

The Science
As you hummed into the tube, you created sound waves. These waves traveled along the inside of the tube. As they passed the cellophane, the sound waves energized the plastic, causing it to vibrate. The vibrations of the plastic generated sound waves. This buzzing noise added to the hum and produced a richer, fuller, and "buzzier" sound.

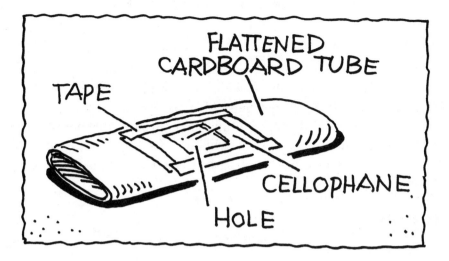

2.20 BOTTLE SOUNDS

Like clarinets and saxophones, flutes are woodwind instruments. The flute's column of air, however, is not set in motion by a vibrating reed. Instead, the flutist must blow across the opening of the mouthpiece. When the stream of air flows through this hole at the right angle, it produces a soft "whistle." As this whistle travels through the instrument's body, it is shaped into the rich, warm tones of a flute.

Materials
* several plastic soft drink containers
* water
* ruler

To Do
Clean and dry an empty soft drink container. Place the neck of the container just below your lower lip. Curl your upper lip outward so that it directs a stream of air at the neck's opening. Vary the force of the air jet (and its angle) until a rich sound is produced by the flowing air.

Fill a second bottle about half full of water. Before you produce a sound with this container, make a guess. Will this note be higher or lower in pitch than the note produced in the empty container? Test your prediction.

CHORD CONNECTION: If you have three identical containers and three friends willing to join in, you can form a pleasing musical chord. Keep one container empty. Fill another container one-fifth full with water. Fill the third container one-third full of water. Play the three notes at the same time. You may have to "tune" the containers slightly. This can be done by adding or removing water.

The Science
As you blew into the bottle, you set the air in motion. As the particles of air moved back and forth, they formed a sound wave. This sound emerged from the neck of the bottle as a distinct note.

Water that was added to the container filled up some of the space. Since the column of air was shortened by the rising level of water, it produced a sound of higher pitch.

2.21 CLINK, CLANK, CLUNK

Doe-ray-me-fah-so-lah-tee-doe. It's the musical scale. Although you may not know it, the scale is built upon a mathematical relationship. This math connection takes you from one note to the next. Suppose an organ pipe that was 20 inches long produced a C note? If you used a pipe three-fourths the length of this one (or 15 inches), it would produce an F note. If you used a pipe three-fifths the length of the C (or 12 inches), it would produce an A note.

Materials
* *several identical drinking glasses*
* *metal spoon*
* *ruler*

To Do
Place a drinking glass on a flat surface. Use a spoon to gently tap the side of the glass. What do you hear? Now place a second glass next to the first. Halfway fill the second glass with water. Before you produce a sound with this half-filled glass, make a guess. Will this note be higher or lower in pitch than the note produced in the empty container? Test your prediction.

MATH CONNECTION: How good are you at fractions? Good enough to make a musical scale? Let's find out.

You can make a scale by filling identical drinking glasses to fixed heights with water. Below is a list showing the height at which the glasses need to be filled in order to create a musical scale.

DON'T FORGET: You'll need to fine tune the pitches by adding or removing water.

Glass filled with water	C note
Glass 8/9 filled with water	D note
Glass 4/5 filled with water	E note
Glass 3/4 filled with water	F note
Glass 2/3 filled with water	G note
Glass 3/5 filled with water	A note

Glass ⁸⁄₁₅ filled with water   B note
Glass ½ filled with water   C note

The Science

When the glass was struck by the spoon, the water and the glass began to vibrate. This back-and-forth motion was transferred to the air that filled the glass. Eventually, these air vibrations reached us as sound. As water was added to the glass, the amount of original vibrating material increased. Since there was more matter to vibrate (water and glass), it produced a lower pitch.

Although the ratios of the note lengths are exact, the shape and material that forms the glass affects the pitch. That's why you had to fine-tune the notes!

2.22 CRYSTAL CLEAR

$\mathbb{T}$rue or false?

Only glasses that are made of expensive crystal will "sing" when their rim is rubbed.

Answer: Find out yourself!

Materials
* inexpensive glass that has slender stem and circular base
* wet fingertips

To Do

Place a glass on a flat tabletop. Wet the tips of your index and middle finger. Place these fingers on the rim of the glass. Use your other hand to secure the base of the glass.

Slowly move your wet fingertips along the edge of the glass. Make sure that they keep a gentle contact with the glass. If the water dries up, wet your fingertips again. The glass rim must remain slick but not soaked. When the contact between your finger and the rim reaches the right tension, the glass will begin to "sing."

Fill the glass halfway with water. Make this glass "sing." How does the sound of this glass differ from the sound of an empty glass? Can you explain your observations?

CAUTION
Do not use a glass that has chips or cracks.

The Science

As you rubbed your finger along the rim, you caused the glass to vibrate. These vibrations were transferred to the air that filled the glass. As the vibrating column of air moved outward, you detected it as a note.

When you added water to the glass, you increased the amount of matter. Both the glass material and water was set in motion when the rim was rubbed. When a greater amount of matter vibrates, a slower back-and-forth movement is produced. This vibration was transferred to the air within the glass and moved outward from the container as a low-pitch sound.

CHECK IT OUT! Why do stemmed glasses "sing" better than glasses that do not have a stem?

2.23 STRING SOUNDS

Tighten. Tighten. Tighten. Loosen. Loosen. Tighten.

Have you ever watched a musician tune a string instrument such as a violin, cello, or guitar? As the tuning head twists, the string's pitch changes. Eventually, the string's tension is perfect and so is the note. Bravo!

Materials
* *wooden board*
* *pushpins*
* *fishing line*
* *small pail*
* *sand, aquarium gravel, or marbles*
* *pencil*

To Do
Press a pushpin into the end of a small wooden board. Position the board so that the end opposite from the pushpin sticks out beyond the edge of a table.

Cut a length of fishing line about 1 foot longer than the board. Loop one end of the line around the pushpin. Tie the free end to the handle of a small pail. Lower the pail off the edge of the board so that it is hanging.

Insert a pencil between the fishing line and board that are near the table's edge. Pluck the string.

Add some sand to the bucket and pluck the string again. Continue adding sand until the bucket is full. What happens to the sound as more sand is added to the bucket?

The Science
The pitch of the plucked string depends upon the tension in the string. As you added sand to the bucket, its weight increased. This added weight caused the tension in the string to increase. When the string was plucked, it produced a higher-pitched sound.

CHECK IT OUT! A pedal steel guitar is an instrument often used in country music. Find out how its pedals alter the sound of its notes.

2.24 PITCH SWITCH

Slide your fingers along a guitar neck and you'll feel ridges. These ridges divide the neck into distinct regions called frets. When the string is pressed, it's vibrating length is determined by the nearest fret. Frets closest to the sound hole produce the highest notes. Frets farthest from the sound hole produce notes of lowest pitch.

Materials
* *paper cup*
* *kite string*
* *tape*
* *ruler*
* *two paper clips*
* *pushpin*

To Do
Use the pushpin to punch a small hole near the center of the cup's bottom. Cut a length of kite string about 2 feet long. Pass the string halfway through the cup hole. Tie the end of the string (on the inner cup side) to the paper clip.

Pull the opposite end of the string so that the paper clip becomes pressed against the inside of the cup bottom. Use tape to secure the cup to one end of the ruler.

Bend the other paper clip into an "S" shape hook. Fasten this hook to the opposite end of the ruler. Use tape to secure.

Tie the free end of the string to the paper clip. The string should be tied so that it is taut and can be "plucked."

Trim away any excess string. Pluck the string. Describe the sound. Press down on the string to force it to contact the ruler. Pluck the string again. What has happened to the sound? Try pressing down at different points along the string. How does the location of the "press" affect the sound?

The Science
When the string was first plucked, it vibrated freely along its entire length. This produced the sound with the lowest pitch. When you pressed down on the string, you shortened the length of the vibrating section. This shorter length produced a higher pitch. By moving this "end point," you varied the pitch of the plucked note.

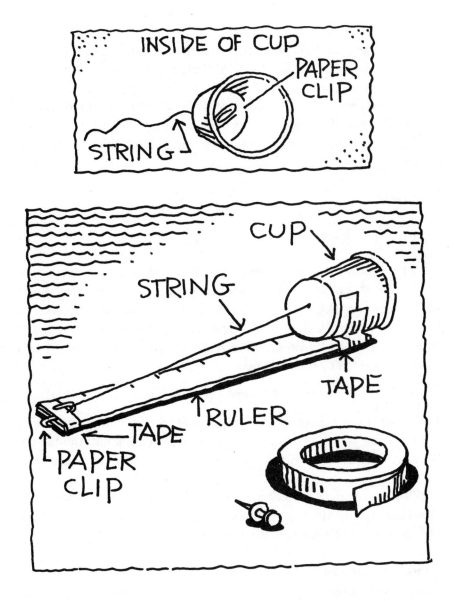

INSIDE OF CUP

PAPER CLIP

STRING

CUP

STRING

TAPE

RULER

TAPE

PAPER CLIP

2.25 A LITTLE SPLASH

Musicians need to stay in tune. That's where a tuning fork comes in. A tuning fork is a piece of metal that, when struck, vibrates at a very exact rate. This rate of vibration is called a *frequency*. Some tuning forks vibrate at the frequency of a C note. Other forks vibrate at the frequencies of other notes. By selecting the correct tuning fork, a musician can tune an instrument to the same pitch that is shared by all band members.

Materials
* *tuning fork*
* *cup filled with water*

NOTE: When striking a tuning fork, hit it against a solid but padded object. Knees, elbows, cloth-covered furniture, or carpeted floors work great. Try not to hit the fork against hard, unpadded objects. A hard strike might bend or distort the shape of the tuning fork. If this happens, the tuning fork may change its vibration and produce a note of different pitch or less volume.

To Do
Firmly hold the tuning fork by its handle. Strike one of the double ends against your knee or padded surface. Keep holding the handle. Do you hear the note? Strike the fork again. Is the note the same or different?

Fill a cup with water. Strike the tuning fork against your knee. Slowly bring the vibrating ends to the water's surface. Touch these ends to the water's surface. What do you observe?

Home Connection
Many home humidifiers use vibrations to produce a mist of water. The humidifier contains a tank of water. The water from tank enters a chamber. Although the top of the chamber is open to the room, the bottom of the chamber houses a vibrating unit. This unit produces a pitch too high for humans to detect (hence, it's called ultrasonic) As this part vibrates, it transfers energy to the surrounding water. The

vibrating water particles absorb enough energy to boost them out of the liquid tank and into the air as a visible mist.

2.26 A BIGGER SOUND

Look at the stage of a rock 'n' roll concert and you're likely to see a wall of speakers. Get close to these speakers and you'll discover that they are big, REALLY BIG. Big speakers have a larger vibrating surface than smaller speakers. This larger surface area can transfer vibrations to many more air particles than a smaller surface area. As the numbers of these vibrating particles increase, so does the volume!

Materials
* tuning fork
* large flat surface (such as a tabletop)
* a friend

To Do
Strike a tuning fork against your knee. Hold it at arm's length. Can you hear the pitch it produces? Have a friend stand across the room. Can he or she also hear the sound of the vibrating fork?

Now strike the tuning fork again. As it vibrates, place the base of the handle firmly against a large flat object, such as a tabletop or chalkboard. What happens now?

Experiment with surfaces of different size and composition. What characteristics make a surface boost the loudness of a sound? What characteristics make an object muffle the loudness of a sound?

The Science
As the tuning fork vibrates, it transfers its vibration energy to the surrounding air particles. As you can see, the arms of the tuning fork are quite small. Therefore, they are not in direct contact with a great deal of particles. Sounds produced solely by the vibrating fork aren't loud.

When the fork is placed against a large surface, such as a tabletop, things change. As the fork continues to vibrate, its vibration is transferred to the tabletop.

Because of its size, the tabletop is in contact with many more air particles than the tuning fork.

As this greater number of particles are set in motion, a much louder sound is produced. As you investigate materials, you'll find that hard surfaces that are free to vibrate are great for boosting sound volumes. In contrast, materials that cannot vibrate are poor boosters of sound.

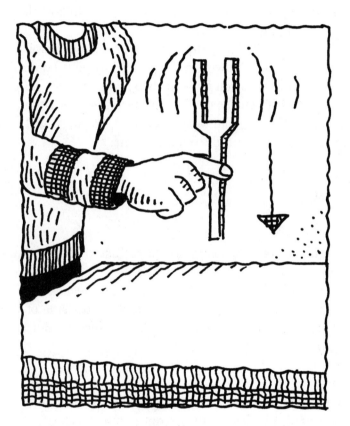

2.27 BONEHEAD SOUNDS

Have you ever listening to a recording of your own voice? If so, were you surprised to hear how it sounded? Most people discover that their recorded voice sounds much different from the voice that they hear when they speak. The difference has to do with how the sound is conducted to your ears.

When you speak, much of your sound is projected outward into the air. A good portion of it, however, is captured by your body. This captured sound vibrates through your body and arrives at your ear through the bones of your head. This through-the-bone sound changes what you detect. Others (and tape recorders), however, will only hear the sound that is transmitted through the air.

Materials
* tuning fork

To Do
Strike the tuning fork against your knee. Listen to the sound. How would you describe its volume and richness?

Strike the tuning fork again. This time, while the fork is still vibrating, firmly press the base of the handle against the side of your jaw. How does pressing the fork against this bone affect the characteristics of the sound?

The Science
When the tuning fork vibrated in air, it transferred its energy to a limited number of air particles. This produced a soft sound.

When the vibrating fork was placed against your jaw, things changed. The vibrations were transferred directly to the jaw bone. This bone vibrated and passed the back-and-forth movement along the bones of your skull. Eventually, this "internal vibration" was transferred to the ear. There, it was detected as sound. Since travel through solid objects, such as bone, is a great way of transferring sound, the volume was boosted.

On Stage Connection

Nowadays, most musicians don't use metal tuning forks. Instead, they have digital tuners that display a readout of the instrument's note in relation to the correct pitch.

When they did use metal tuning forks, they had a trick for hearing the note above the background noise of the orchestra. After striking the double end of the tuning fork, the musician bit onto the handle of the fork. The sound was transferred directly from the fork to the teeth to the jaw to the skull to the ear parts. No matter how loud the orchestra was, this internal sound had a greater volume!

2.28 SING WITH ME

IHave you ever sung in the shower? If so, did some notes sound much louder than others? By varying your pitch, you can uncover notes that the room seems to boost. This amplification is a natural effect that is caused by the shape of the bathroom space. When you hit the right note, the walls seem to join in and vibrate with your voice!

Materials
* two empty and identical soft drink containers
* a friend

To Do
Place a soft drink container on a flat surface. Have a friend hold the other container several feet away. Instruct your friend to blow into the container to produce a low-pitched whistle.

After the whistle has sounded for several seconds, position your ear near the opening of the other container. What do you hear? How long does it last? Who started this tone?

The Science
When your friend blew into the soft drink container, he or she produced a steady pitch. As this sound traveled outward from the "played" container, its waves struck the empty container. The empty container began to vibrate.

Since both containers were identical, they had the same built-in "pitch." When struck by the "tuned" sound waves, the unplayed container responded and began to vibrate. The vibration was strong enough to produce a back-and-forth movement of the air trapped within this unplayed bottle. Soon, both bottles were producing the same pitch.

2.29 VIBRATING TOGETHER

Imagine being in a room where several people are playing musical instruments. In the corner sits an unplayed piano. The music builds in intensity, filling the room with a loud and rich sound. Then the music ends abruptly. The piano, however, plays on. Although no one sits at the instrument, the piano produces a note that seems to fit in with the last note played by the musicians. Ghosts? No, resonance.

Materials
* *guitar, piano, or other stringed instrument*

To Do
Strum an open guitar string or play any key on the piano. Listen and memorize the pitch. You may have to sing with the note in order to produce its exact pitch. Practice until you can reproduce the same note.

Stop the instrument's string from vibrating. Once the string is stationary, sing out your note in a loud and steady tone for several seconds. Direct your voice at the sound box, sound board, or string itself.

Abruptly stop singing. Listen. What do you hear? Can you tell which string is vibrating? How can you be sure?

The Science
By listening and reproducing the instrument's sound, you tuned your voice to the pitch of the vibrating string. When you touched the vibrating string, its movement was stopped. Your voice, however, produced a note that was "tuned" to the string.

When the vibrations of your voice struck the instrument's strings, they set in motion any strings that had the same built-in frequency. Even though it wasn't plucked or strummed, the original string started to vibrate. Once it started, it had enough energy to continue vibrating on its own.

2.30 LISTENING TO THE BEAT

"**O**uch! That is cold! Where did you get that thing? From the fridge?"

A physician's stethoscope is a sound-capturing device. Its sound gathering end is formed by a flat drumhead. Sounds detected by this surface are transferred through the hose to the broadcasting end of the tool. There, vibrations leave the tube and are detected by the physician's ear.

Materials

* two funnels
* 1-foot-long plastic tubing

CAUTION

Never place any object inside your ear! In this experiment, the funnel is placed around your outer ear.

To Do

Slip each end of the plastic tubing over the spout end of a funnel. To test your device, place one of the funnels against the wall. The rim of the funnel opening should lie flat on the wall's surface. Place the opening of the other funnel around your ear. Gently tap on the wall. What do you hear?

Now place one of the funnels over your heart. Make sure that the rim lies flat against your skin. Move the other funnel to your ear. What do you hear?

Keep listening. Take a deep breath. Can you hear the air as it travels along the passageways of your lungs?

The Science

Your heart is a powerful muscle. As this muscle contracts, it pumps blood through the vessels of your body. To ensure that the pumped blood follows a one-way route, valves shut off and block the return flow of blood. The closure of these valves within the heart produces the sound we call a heartbeat. As this vibration travels through the body, it spreads out. The large collector of the stethoscope detects and concentrates these sounds. At the ear, the vibrations are detected as sound.

2.31 GLASSES FOR HEARING

Did you know that windows talk? Yak, yak, yak and yak. Well, not exactly. But surfaces, such as windows, vibrate to the beat of a person's voice. Several years ago, it was discovered that spies monitored the vibration of windows by using high-tech equipment. Although the movement was very slight, it could be detected by a beam of laser light. By analyzing the reflected beam, the equipment could distinguish words that were spoken in secrecy.

Materials
* *drinking glass*
* *wall*
* *radio*

To Do
Find a solid wall that divides two rooms. Place a radio in one room with the volume set to a very soft level. Shut the door and go into the adjoining room.

Place a drinking glass against the wall. The rim of the glass should lie flat against the wall. While holding the glass, place your ear against the base of the glass. What do you hear?

Move your listening device to other parts of the wall. Do some areas transmit louder sounds?

The Science
The radio produced sound waves that traveled outward into the room. These waves struck the wall and produced very tiny vibrations. In the adjoining room, the vibrations could not be detected without the drinking glass. Although the wall was moving back and forth, its movement was too small to produce a detectable sound wave.

By placing the drinking glass against the wall, the "air wave" was not needed. Instead, the wall's movement was transferred directly to the glass. From there, the vibrations traveled directly to the ear and were interpreted as sound.

2.32 BIG BOOMER

Jet aircrafts do it. Fireworks do it. But did you realize that you can also create a huge boom in the privacy of your own living room?

Materials
* corrugated cardboard (from a shipping box)
* brown paper
* pair of scissors
* ruler
* tape

To Do
Cut out a triangle from brown paper. The triangle should measure 14 inches × 14 inches × 20 inches.

Cut a square of corrugated cardboard. The square should measure 12 inches on a side. Use your scissors to score a straight line from one corner to the opposite corner of the square. Make sure that you only score the surface and do not cut completely through the cardboard.

Place the brown paper on a flat surface. Place the cardboard over it as shown in the illustration (with scored-side up). Fold over the edge of the brown paper and secure it to the cardboard with tape.

Pick up this clapper device. Fold it away from the score line, so that the paper folds inside the closed cardboard halves.

Hold the free end of the clapper overhead. Fling your arm down as fast as possible. What do you hear?

The Science
As your arm dropped, the clapper opened. Air that rushed in to fill the opening space moved fast enough to create a shock wave. Although this boom was smaller than the shock waves made by supersonic jets, it was formed in a similar way.

The crack of a whip is also caused by a shock wave. The whip crack breaks the sound barrier. A snap of the wrist produces a wave that travels down the whip. As the wave moves, it increases in speed. By the time it reaches the tip, it is traveling faster than the speed of sound. This creates a shock wave that we hear as the whip crack.

CHECK IT OUT! Find out more about the supersonic transport, the Concorde, that carries passengers across the Atlantic Ocean.

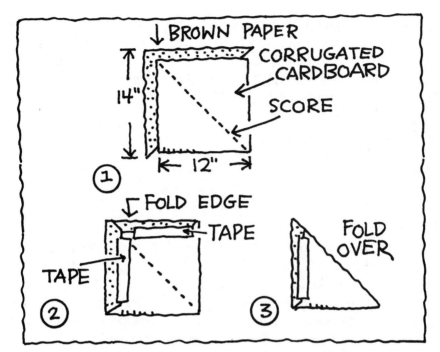

2.33 ANCIENT RECORDINGS

Long ago (in what may now seem like prehistoric times), there were no cassettes or CDs. In order to listen to music, people had to play weird things called phonograph records. Unlike a tape, which uses magnetic data, or a CD, which uses digital pits, these recordings were "cut" into a plastic material called vinyl.

Materials
* discarded phonograph record
* turntable
* tape
* heavy stock paper
* needle
* hand lens

To Do
Use your hand lens to examine the record grooves. Are the groves straight or wavy? Do they have a regular or changing pattern? Are they all the same thickness?

Since this is a discarded record, place a fingernail in one of the grooves. Slowly move your fingernail around the record. How does it feel? Do you hear any sounds forming at your fingernail?

Wrap a large sheet of heavy stock paper into a cone. Secure the shape with tape. Flatten out the cone's pointed end. Fold about an inch of the end back onto the cone. Use a piece of tape to secure the fold. Insert a needle into the flap as shown in the illustration.

Place an old record on a turntable. Spin the turntable by hand and place the needle lightly into one of the grooves. What happens?

HINT
If you don't have a turntable, you can substitute a spinning kitchen tray known as a "Lazy Susan."

The Science
A record's grooves have a shape that stores a sound recording. The groove's closely packed wavy walls produce high pitches. Grooves with spread-out waves produce lower pitches.

In order to hear these "etchings," the plastic patterns must be changed into air vibrations. When a needle traveled through the groove, it vibrated with these etched waves. The needle's movement was transferred to the paper cone. The cone vibrated and transferred its movement to a large and detectable volume of air.

CHECK IT OUT! What happens to a record's pitch when the turntable speeds up?

2.34 SPACE VOICE

In space, no one can hear any sort of sound! In order to transfer sound you need matter. And, for the most part, space is empty.

Speaking of space, this next device makes some strange, far-out sounds. It also changes the quality of your voice. Just listen.

Materials
* metal coil toy
* kite string
* two paper clips
* two paper cups
* pair of scissors

To Do
Cut two lengths of kite string, each about 6 inches long. Tie a paper clip to one end of each string. Punch a small hole in the bottom of a paper cup. Pass the string through the hole so that the paper clip remains on the inside of the cup.

Tie the free end of one string to the end loop of a metal coil. Tie the free end of the other string to the loop on the coil's opposite end.

Put some tension in the coil by gently pulling it apart. Don't over-stretch the coil!

Talk into one cup while your friend listens in the other cup. Then exchange roles. Can you hear the other person's voice? How does the coil affect the sound?

The Science
When you spoke, you produced vibrations of air particles. These vibrations were collected by the cup. The movements traveled down the string and struck the coil. Not all of the vibrations emerged from the opposite end of the coil. Some of the vibrations bounced back and forth within the coil. As they rebounded, some of the sounds were transferred to the distant cup. These lagging sounds produced the weird echo-like effect.

CHECK IT OUT! How does changing the tension in the coil affect the quality of the sound?

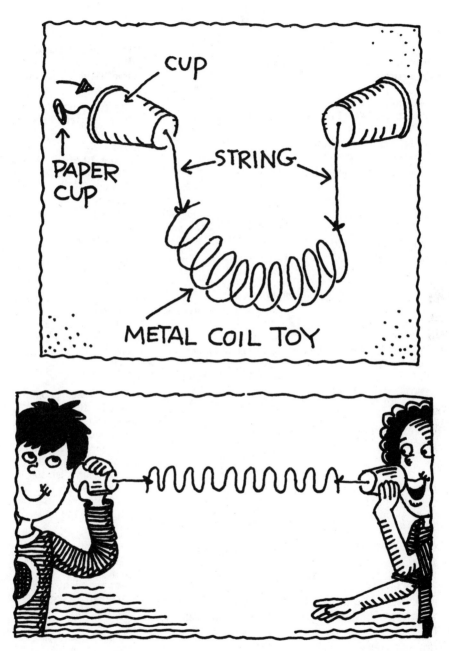

INDEX

ANSWERS TO CHECK IT OUT!

p. 10 White light that was separated into colors by the CD surface; p. 16 Floating oil forms a layer thin enough to separate white light into its component colors; p. 42 Creates a new pattern of colored chips; p. 62 Difficult, but can be done with plenty of patience and practice; p. 74 The retina; p. 77 Upside down and larger; p. 79 Completely out of the shadow; p. 81 The lens must be held at a distance from the object and your eye; p. 87 The horse runs backward; p. 90 Loud sounds make the grains jump higher; p. 119 Better, the particles in metal are packed more closely together than those in string; p. 121 Plastic covering will dampen the sound; p. 123 Larger cup makes louder sound; p. 133 The stem allows the cup to vibrate more freely; p. 134 Pedals change the tension and pitch of string; p. 153 A needle-nosed, stream-lined jet that crosses the Atlantic Ocean at supersonic speed; p. 155 Pitch gets higher.

ABOUT THE AUTHOR

MICHAEL ANTHONY DISPEZIO is a renaissance educator who teaches, writes, and conducts teacher workshops throughout the world. He received an M.A. in biology from Boston University, and for six summers was a research assistant to Nobel laureate Albert Szent-Gyorgyi.

After tiring of counting hairs on copepods, Michael traded the marine science laboratory for the classroom. Over the years, he has taught physics, chemistry, earth science, general science, mathematics, and rock 'n' roll musical theater.

To date, Michael is the author of *Critical Thinking Puzzles, Great Critical Thinking Puzzles, Challenging Critical Thinking Puzzles, Visual Thinking Puzzles, Awesome Experiments in Electricity and Magnetism,* and *Awesome Experiments in Force and Motion* (all from Sterling). He is also the co-author of eighteen elementary, middle, and high school science textbooks and has been a "hired creative-gun" for clients including The Weather Channel and Children's Television Workshop. He also develops activities for the classroom guides to *Discover* magazine and *Scientific American Frontiers.*

Michael was a contributor to the National Science Teachers Association's Pathways to Science Standards. This document set offers guidelines for moving the national science standards from vision to practice. Michael's work with the NSTA has also included authoring the critically acclaimed NSTA curriculum, *The Science of HIV.*